ARGONAUT PRESS #10

A SPANISH VOYAGE TO VANCOUVER AND THE NORTH-WEST COAST OF AMERICA

EDITED BY
CECIL JANE

N. ISRAEL / AMSTERDAM
DA CAPO PRESS / NEW YORK

Printed in Western Germany

Published 1971

by

N. Israel / Keizersgracht 539 / Amsterdam - C.

&

Da Capo Press
- a division of Plenum Publishing Corporation -
227 West 17th Street / New York 10011

ISBN 90 6072 111 x
ISBN 90 6072 701 0

CELEBRATIONS AT THE COMING OF AGE OF THE DAUGHTER OF MACUINA

A SPANISH VOYAGE TO VANCOUVER
AND THE
NORTH-WEST COAST OF AMERICA

BEING THE

NARRATIVE OF THE VOYAGE MADE IN THE YEAR 1792
BY THE SCHOONERS *SUTIL* AND *MEXICANA* TO
EXPLORE THE STRAIT OF FUCA

Translated from the Spanish
with an *Introduction*
BY
CECIL JANE

Illustrated with a folding map
and six illustrations

1930
THE ARGONAUT PRESS
EMPIRE HOUSE, 175 PICCADILLY
LONDON

A SPANISH VOYAGE TO VANCOUVER
AND THE
NORTH-WEST COAST OF AMERICA

GENERAL EDITOR: N. M. PENZER, M.A., F.R.G.S.

PREFACE

IN accordance with its programme, the Argonaut Press, in the present publication, is not confining its activities to the reprinting of travels of men whose names have become household words. In presenting the work of a nameless Spanish author of the late eighteenth century, it is not only bringing to the notice of scholars a work that has never been before translated into English, but is reprinting the account of a voyage of very considerable geographical importance. Narratives of voyages to discover a North-West Passage from the Atlantic side are familiar to all, but the efforts of the Spaniards to find such a passage from the Pacific are much less known.

The account of the expedition of the schooners *Sutil* and *Mexicana* to the north-west coast of America was printed in 1802 by Martin Fernandez de Navarrete. The narrative is anonymous, but internal evidence suffices to prove that it was written by one of the officers attached to the expedition, and that this officer was in the *Sutil*. There is some reason for thinking that this unknown officer was probably the cartographer attached to that vessel.

Navarrete prefaced his edition with a lengthy introduction which has been here summarised. His purpose was very largely to answer the attacks made by certain French writers upon the conduct of the Spanish explorers and to defend his fellow-countrymen against the charge of having invented voyages and of having exaggerated their contributions to the advance of knowledge. In actual fact, there is no doubt that for their share in exploring the north-western coast of the continent, the Spaniards deserve the very greatest credit, and that more especially in the case of their later expeditions, their aim was rather altruistic than selfish.

The Argonaut Press is greatly indebted to Messrs. Maggs Bros. for the loan of the rare original Spanish edition of the work.

N. M. PENZER.

CONTENTS

	PAGE
PREFACE	v
INTRODUCTION	ix

CHAPTER I
The expedition of the schooners *Sutil* and *Mexicana* for the exploration of Juan de Fuca Strait proposed to the Count of Revillagigedo, Viceroy of New Spain ... 3

CHAPTER II
Voyage from Acapulco to Nootka Sound ... 11

CHAPTER III
Ships in the harbour of Nootka ... 16

CHAPTER IV
The schooners leave Nootka, and are forced back into harbour by the bad weather ... 21

CHAPTER V
Don Salvador Fidalgo proposes to form a settlement at Nuñez Gaona, similar to that at Nootka ... 26

CHAPTER VI
Account of the harbour of Córdoba ... 38

CHAPTER VII
In the morning the schooners reach this closed passage ... 43

CHAPTER VIII
The schooners leave Descanso Creek ... 52

CHAPTER IX
Valdes goes in the launch and explores Tabla and Arco channels and the entrances near ... 60

CHAPTER X
Parting from the English vessels ... 64

CHAPTER XI
Difficulty caused by contrary currents near Refuge Creek ... 70

CHAPTER XII
The schooners leave and pass through the Channel of New Whirlpools ... 74

CHAPTER XIII
The schooners set out and proceed along the channel of Descubierta, in which they anchor ... 82

CONTENTS

CHAPTER XIV
 Stay of the schooners in Guemes Harbour — PAGE 85

CHAPTER XV
 Reflections on the slight practical value of the explorations made — 89

CHAPTER XVI
 Nautical information and description of Nootka Sound and Island — 94

CHAPTER XVII
 The Inhabitants of Nootka — 98

CHAPTER XVIII
 Continuation of the information gained concerning the manners and customs of the inhabitants of Nootka. — 105

CHAPTER XIX
 Continuation of the account of the Nutkeños. — 115

CHAPTER XX
 The schooners leave Nootka; the wind drives them out to sea, and they are unable to approach the land until they reach 47° north — 122

CHAPTER XXI
 Further information acquired at Monterey — 130

CHAPTER XXII
 The schooners leave Monterey, and owing to bad weather are unable to survey the coast until they arrive at the channel of Santa Barbara, the islands in which they examine — 135

INDEX — 139

MAPS AND ILLUSTRATIONS

Celebrations at the Coming of Age of the Daughter of Macuina	*Frontispiece*	
Map illustrating the Voyage of the *Sutil* and the *Mexicana*	*facing page*	3
Macuina	page	14
Tetacú	,,	30
Maria	,,	31
Praying-room of Macuina	,,	103
Carved Board found at Canal de la Tabla	,,	131

INTRODUCTION

Belief in the existence of a strait, uniting the Atlantic with that sea in which lay the Spice Islands and affording a far shorter and more convenient route to the riches of the East, was very prevalent in the period immediately following the discovery of the New World. Columbus himself, on his last voyage, directed his attention to the search for such a passage; he would appear to have been convinced that it was to be found in the neighbourhood of the Isthmus of Panama. The fallacy of this view was, indeed, presently demonstrated as the character of Central America became better known, but almost at the same time the discovery of the Pacific by Vasco Nuñez de Balboa served to intensify the desire to find a route from one ocean to the other.

The search for this route was prosecuted in various directions. On the eastern coast of America, exploration, with this end in view, culminated to the southward in the expedition of Ferdinand Magellan which proved that there was a way from the Atlantic to the Pacific, but which proved also that this way was so lengthy and so perilous as hardly to be preferable to that route to India which had long before been opened by Vasco da Gama and his successors. It is probable enough that this fact contributed to accentuate efforts to discover a strait to the northward. At an earlier date, Cortés had dispatched vessels in this direction and they had proceeded along the coast from Florida to Newfoundland, but here the work of exploration was practically abandoned by the Spaniards and passed into the hands of English, French, Dutch and Danes, by whom the most important discoveries were made.

It was to the search from the western side that the attention of the Spaniards was directed. They availed themselves of their control of Central America and Mexico to investigate the character of the eastern shores of the Pacific, and to them were primarily due the earliest accounts of that region. No sooner had Cortés established himself in Mexico than he instructed his lieutenants to undertake the exploration of the western coast of that country; he proceeded to build ships for this purpose and endeavoured to obtain a commission from Charles V securing to him a monopoly of the right to explore. Despite the ill-success which attended the first efforts made, those efforts were not abandoned, personal, as well as political and economic, factors leading to their continuance. Nuño de Guzman had established himself in Sinaloa, and he there showed an inclination to deny the superior authority of the conqueror of Mexico, who for his part regarded all that lay to the north as falling within his own preserve. It was primarily to place a check upon the activities of Guzman that Cortés sent Diego Hurtado de Mendoza with three vessels to explore the coast in 1532. The expedition, which effected the annexation of the islands off the coast of Tepic, known as Las Tres Marias, and which reached a point somewhat farther north, was, however, disastrous. Sickness among his crews and shortage of provisions obliged Mendoza to send one ship home; his own vessel was lost with all hands, and the third, having put into a harbour, was abandoned, half her crew being arrested by Guzman and the other half almost exterminated by hostile Indians, only a few survivors reaching the district of Colima. An expedition, commanded by Diego Becerra and Hernando de Grijalva, in the following year was also unfortunate. The two ships of which it was composed were parted in a storm, and Grijalva, after discovering the islands of Socorro and San Benedito, returned home. Becerra was murdered by some mutineers, who themselves perished at the hands of the Indians. The remainder of the crew, with their ship and all their belongings, were seized by Guzman, an act of open hostility which determined Cortés to proceed in person to the north and to assert his authority in that region.

The expedition which he commanded consisted of a force which was to advance by land and three ships which were to support this force from the sea, but the results attained were inconsiderable. After the Gulf of California had been reached, one vessel was wrecked and another burned, while the third was in such poor condition as to make a continuance of the voyage impossible. As Cortés had learned that Mendoza had arrived in Mexico as viceroy, he decided that his presence was required at home, and therefore abandoned the expedition. At the same time, he was far from proposing to relinquish all further effort to explore the north-west coast. On the contrary, he dispatched Francisco de Ulloa to make discoveries in this region. But the misfortunes which had attended previous attempts continued; one ship was lost in a storm, one after reaching the Isla de Cedros, off the west coast of Lower California, returned to Acapulco, and the third, in which was Ulloa, continuing the voyage, was never heard of again.

INTRODUCTION

The degree of success attained by these expeditions had thus, perhaps, been hardly commensurate with the effort made and with the expense involved. The Pacific coast of Mexico had, indeed, been more or less thoroughly explored and California had been discovered, but the lands which had been reached seemed to be of no great value. More especially, no trace had been found of that developed civilisation which had been reported to exist to the north of Mexico, and still less had anything been learned of "Cebola," the mythical city of fabulous wealth which had been described by the Franciscan, Fray Marcós de Nixa. Despite such disappointment, however, exploration was continued under the auspices of the viceroys of Mexico, and while Hernando de Alarcon entered the Colorado River, Juan Rodriguez Ceballos reached the coast of Upper California and in some measure, at least, anticipated the later discoveries of Drake.

One cause which served to lead to continuance of effort was the development of trade between the Philippines and Mexico, which made it desirable that some harbour should be found on the north-west coast to serve as a port of call for ships coming from Manilla. But a far stronger motive for exploration was the currency of reports that at no great distance to the north there was a strait uniting the two oceans. At a very early date, Alvar Nuñez Cabeza de Vaca had declared that such a passage existed, and had at least suggested that he had reached it on his march from Florida to Mexico. In the first half of the sixteenth century a story was told of some Portuguese navigators who had passed from China to Lisbon through this mythical strait of "Anian," and who had accomplished the journey in the surprisingly short period of forty-five days. In succeeding years, other similar stories were told. Andres de Urdaneta would appear to have expressed to Philip II his conviction of the existence of a strait to the north of Florida, and through this same strait Lorenzo Ferrer Maldonado was alleged to have sailed. At a later date Juan de Fuca was credited with having been dispatched to fortify the western entrance to the passage between the two oceans, and he was currently believed to have found that entrance and to have given to it his own name. In the first half of the seventeenth century Bartolomé Fonte was supposed to have found men from Boston who had penetrated into the heart of the continent by a tortuous route which had an outlet on the west.

Confirmation of these stories of an inter-oceanic passage was thought to be supplied by the appearance of Drake and Cavendish on the Pacific coast. It was held to be impossible that they could have rounded the continent to the south, and it was therefore argued that they must have come through the strait of "Anian." This supposition afforded an additional ground for the further prosecution of exploration along the coast to the north-west. It became desirable on military, no less than upon economic grounds, to discover the entrance of the passage in order that it might be seized and fortified so as to prevent further hostile raids upon the Pacific coast. Of the many expeditions consequently dispatched, the most important was perhaps the second voyage of Sebastian Vizcaino, who discovered the harbour of Monterey and reached Cape Mendocino. But the fact that the degree of success attained was relatively small caused attention to be directed rather to expeditions by land, and the work of exploration, no less than that of conversion, was to a great extent left in the hands of Jesuits, by whom missions were established in California. It had, indeed, gradually become clear that if any strait did exist, it could only be in such high latitudes that its navigation was likely to be impeded by ice and that its economic value would thus be somewhat dubious.

A great renewal of activity, however, marked the reign of Charles III. By that time the fur trade had developed, and in it ships of various nations were engaged, while the advance of the Russians in Siberia seemed to threaten an attempt on their part to extend their dominion to the American continent. Spanish interests, therefore, seemed to demand that more attention should be paid to the north-west coast, while at the same time the enthusiasm of the king for every extension of scientific knowledge supplied an additional motive for the active resumption of the work of exploration. A number of expeditions were accordingly dispatched to this region in the second half of the eighteenth century. Joseph de Galves effected the establishment of a military station at Monterey, the idea of which had been mooted soon after its discovery by Vizcaino; missions under the direction of the fathers of San Fernando at Mexico were created in the neighbourhood. A few years later Juan Perez reached Nootka Sound, while an expedition under the command of Bruno Eceta, Juan de Ayala and Juan de la Bodega made important geographical investigations, the results of which proved to be serviceable to Captain Cook when he later arrived in the same region. An establishment was set up at Nootka Sound, and when the Spanish position there was disputed by the English and threatened by the Russians, Francisco Eliza was sent with three men-of-war to put the station in a posture of defence.

The purpose of the Spanish expeditions at this time, however, was in general rather scientific than political or economic; they were primarily intended to advance geographical knowledge by the production of more accurate maps, and to verify or disprove the accounts given by earlier voyagers. Thus when currency was again given to the story of the supposed discoveries of Maldonado, the corvettes *Descubierta* and *Atrevida* were sent to investigate its truth. They carefully surveyed the coast from Cape Engaño to Cape St. Bartholomew, incidentally determining the height of Mount Edgcumbe and afterwards of Mount St. Elias. They explored Behring Bay and Mulgrave Sound, and examined every inlet which might possibly be the western entrance of the strait supposed to have been found by Maldonado. The result of their voyage was to prove that the story was wholly fictitious, as the unreality of the alleged strait of Juan de Fuca was finally demonstrated by the expedition of the *Sutil* and *Mexicana*, described in the present volume. It was characteristic of the somewhat altruistic nature of these expeditions that their leaders readily communicated the results attained to the commanders of vessels belonging to other nations and engaged upon similar work. By the close of the eighteenth century, the north-western coast had been mapped with some approach to completeness as far north as the extreme point of Vancouver Island, and it had been finally established that there was no passage uniting Nootka Sound or any other western inlet with Hudson's Bay, with some arm of the sea to the east.

The history of these Spanish expeditions falls into three periods. In the first, which extended to the middle of the seventeenth century, the results attained were disappointing, largely owing to the absence of any very coherent plan and to lack of knowledge of the provision required for exploration in high latitudes. They did, however, serve to illustrate the perseverance and the intrepidity of those who engaged upon them. The second period may be dated from the time of Pedro Porter y Casanate, and was devoted less to the making of further discoveries than to the consolidation of the position of Spain in the area already visited. For the purpose of assisting the trade between Manila and the viceroyalty of Mexico, the department of San Blas had been formed, and it had been hoped that the port here created would be suitable both for the repair of vessels putting into it and for the construction of new ships. The supply of suitable timber was, however, found to be deficient, while the character of the neighbouring Indian tribes threatened a state of constant hostility. Some more suitable position was accordingly sought, and the successive establishment of posts along the Californian coast, of which Monterey was the most important, was an indication of the desire to facilitate the development of trade in this region. At the same time, however, attention was devoted to the task of converting and civilising the natives, and Vancouver bears witness to the success which crowned the efforts of the fathers in this region. The excellent relations which generally subsisted between the Spaniards and the Indians suffices, indeed, to disprove the charge that the sole aim of the former was to exploit the latter. In the last period, which begins with the reign of Charles III, while attention was devoted to meeting the danger of Russian aggression and to developing the trade with the Philippines, the interrupted work of exploration was resumed. In the closing years of the eighteenth century, Spanish navigators played an honourable and important part in the development of knowledge, and by their almost single-hearted devotion to the cause of civilisation and science afforded, perhaps, an interesting contrast to the seamen of other nations, whose attention was far more concentrated upon the acquisition of wealth from the bartering of furs.

A SPANISH VOYAGE TO VANCOUVER
AND THE NORTH-WEST COAST OF AMERICA

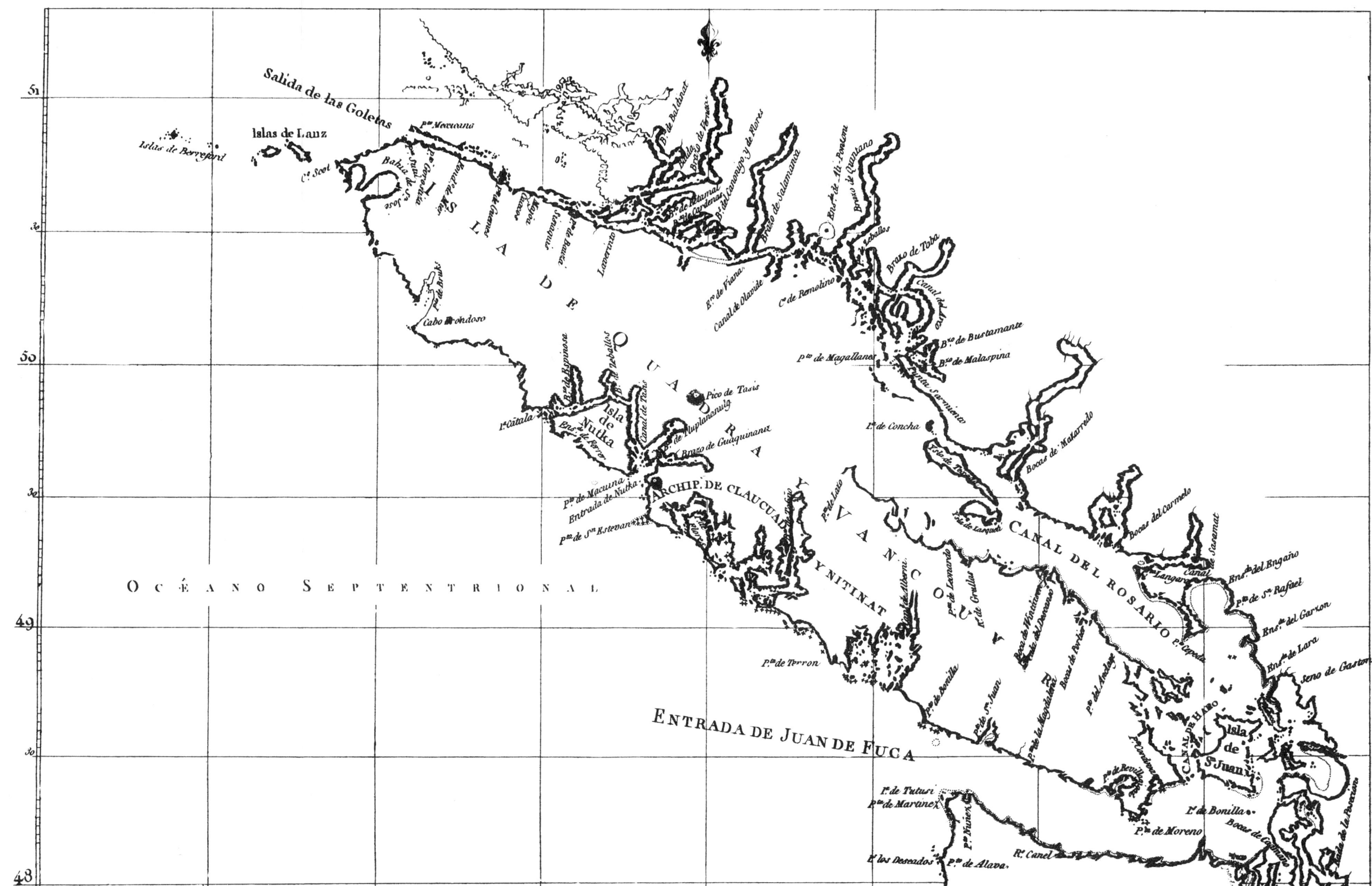

MAP ILLUSTRATING THE VOYAGE OF THE "SUTIL" AND "MEXICANA"

CHAPTER I

The expedition of the schooners *Sutil* and *Mexicana* for the exploration of Juan de Fuca Strait proposed to the Count of Revillagigedo, viceroy of New Spain.—These vessels proceed from Puerto de San Blas to Acapulco to secure the aid of the corvettes *Descubierta* and *Atrevida*; they are delayed and on their arrival do not find the corvettes.—Defects of the schooners.—Efforts made to effect essential improvements.—Assistance rendered by the viceroy to the expedition.—They are made ready to sail.—Their condition and equipment.

Down to the year 1789, the only information which we possessed of Juan de Fuca Strait was the confused account of its discovery in 1592, left by the Greek pilot who gave it his name. Don Estéban Martinez, ensign in the navy, when he was in Nootka after having taken possession of that harbour in the name of His Majesty, related that in 1774, on his return from his expedition to the north, he sighted what appeared to be a very wide sound at 48° 20′ north, and that, thinking that this might be the entry discovered by Fuca, he sent a second pilot, in command of the schooner *Gertrudis*, to ascertain whether or no the strait existed. The pilot eventually returned with the report that he had found an entry, twenty-one miles broad, the middle point of which lay at 48° 30′ north and 19° 28′ west of San Blas.

These reports were transmitted to the government, and Don Francisco Eliza, lieutenant in the navy, was ordered in 1790 to arrange for a detailed examination of this entry. He commissioned a naval ensign, Don Manuel Quimper, commanding the *balandra*, *Princesa Real*, to undertake this. This officer set sail from Nootka Sound, 31 May, explored Claucuad Sound and then spent some time within Fuca Strait visiting some harbours and part of the coast and charting it. He returned, 1 August, the weather preventing further prosecution of the work.

In the following year, Eliza was ordered by the viceroy of New Spain to complete the investigation which he had begun and by which the curiosity of geographers had been aroused. The officer, having under his command the packet-boat *San Carlos* and the schooner *Horcasitas*, left Nootka with the intention of proceeding to 60° north and of then working southwards, examining the coast to Fuca Strait, which he proposed to enter in order to make a complete survey of it. For a long while, however, the winds prevented him from sailing northwards, and he resolved to begin his investigation at 48° north and entered the strait on 27 May. He remained in it until 7 August, when he was forced to leave it owing to an outbreak of scurvy among his crews and to lack of suitable food for them. During the time which he spent there, he caused some harbours to be charted, and the pilot, Don Joseph Narvaez, was sent by him to examine an inlet, as he was unable himself to undertake this work owing to illness.

On his return to Nootka, he wrote an account of his voyage to the viceroy of New Spain, and in the course of the comments which he made, remarked: "Your Excellency may rest assured that the passage to the ocean, for which foreign nations have sought with so much zeal, lies, if it exists at all, nowhere save in this great channel."

These reports were transmitted to His Majesty, and as he was always anxious to advance scientific knowledge and to extend hydrographical information, he at once sent orders to the viceroy of New Spain that appropriate means should be taken to effect such an exploration of Fuca Strait as to resolve all doubts concerning its extent. The Count of Revillagigedo immediately appointed Don Francisco Maurell, lieutenant of frigates, to execute this commission, employing for the purpose the schooner *Sutil* and a frigate's launch.

At this moment there arrived at Acapulco His Majesty's corvettes *Descubierta* and *Atrevida*, engaged in making a voyage round the world, the preliminary of which was to be a search for the supposed passage to the Atlantic, of which the western entrance, according to the well-known account given by Captain Lorenzo Ferrer Maldonado, lay at 59° 30′ north on the north-west coast of North America.

The adverse winds which the commander of the corvettes had experienced on the coast had prevented him from examining any interesting features of it. He could not abandon the main purpose of his commission in order to determine the exact position of some points, since to do so would detain him and would cause him to consume in this way the time set aside for carrying out investigations of much greater importance and interest; for the discharge of his commission five years were required, despite the postponement of some part of it, which could be performed later, and of the determination of the position of points which lay within certain well-defined limits. The ultimate result of this work was to be that the shores of our overseas dominions were to be mapped on a geometrical system analogous to that which had been adopted in the case of our peninsula, its islands, the Canaries and the

Azores, to the great advantage of navigation and to the honour of the Spanish nation.

Calms and contrary winds had forced him to abandon any attempt to examine the coast lying between Sonsonate and Acapulco, before she sailed to the north-west coast, and obstacles of a different kind eventually precluded him from examining the entry visited in 1775 by Don Bruno de Eceta, lieutenant in the navy, or from finding the river of Martin del Aguilar. He had, however, been able to determine the position of Santa Barbara Channel, as well as that of some of the islands formed by it, the result being that the situation of these islands was found to be very different from that of islands already visited, a further examination being thus necessary in order to fix their true position.

For the exploration of the coast from Sonsonate to Acapulco, the viceroy had been asked to detail the schooner *Mexicana*, which was under construction in the department of San Blas. Don Juan Vernaci, lieutenant of frigates, was to proceed in her to chart that part of coast and also the gulf of Amapala. As, however, the second object mainly demanded his attention, and as this could be combined with the continuation of the survey of Juan de Fuca Strait, the commander proposed to the viceroy that this work should be undertaken by officers belonging to his command, who should be supplied with clocks and other instruments required for its adequate performance. As a result, although the schooner *Sutil* and the launch were almost ready on 1 December to undertake their voyage immediately, following the coast and sheltering in harbours along it, until the weather was favourable, the viceroy, for the best reasons, agreed to the suggestion made, being convinced of the advantages of the plan proposed to him.

The choice of ships for the expedition fell on the schooners *Sutil* and *Mexicana*, since it was held that these vessels combined the advantage of light draught, which would protect them against the danger of grounding when navigating channels of little depth and which would enable them to be more easily refloated if they should run aground, with that of handiness under sail or when rowed. In Acapulco they were regarded as better suited for the work than any other vessels which could be procured in the department of San Blas, on the score of their greater seaworthiness. This opinion was communicated to the viceroy, who signified his approval of their selection and also of the appointment of the officers for the expedition, these officers being the captains of frigates, Don Dionisio Alcalá Galiano and Don Cayetano Valdés, and Don Juan Vernaci and Don Secundino Salamanca, lieutenants of frigates.

An order was immediately dispatched to the department of San Blas that the schooners should be sent down to Acapulco without delay, but their arrival at that port was postponed owing to the inclemency of the season, as a result of which fevers among the settlers had assumed the proportions of an epidemic. As the weather became exceptionally favourable for the plan of operations designed by the commander of the corvettes, he left Acapulco for the Philippine Islands on 20 December, eight days before the arrival of the schooners, leaving behind him all that he considered to be useful for the equipment of those vessels. The commander of the corvettes believed that the schooners would be already provided with those supplies for which we had asked in a note sent by Don Juan de la Bodega y Quadra, captain in the navy, to the commandant of the department of San Blas. In this note, we had laid down all that we thought to be necessary in the matter of supplies and outfit, even in event of our modifying the equipment of the ships, were that found to be advisable.

As soon as the schooners reached Acapulco we proceeded to overhaul them, and the first point which came to our notice was their defective construction, the outcome of shortage of material. The source of greatest concern was the fact that even the slight buffeting which they had experienced in the short voyage from San Blas to Acapulco had reduced the size of the hold, with the result that it was impossible to store the supplies of food and drink necessary for the voyage. If the course of hugging the coast and taking in new supplies at the first opportunity were not to be adopted, a method impracticable for many vessels owing to the adverse currents and winds from the north and north-west, which had generally much strength, the preferable course was necessarily to make out to sea, steering north-east, and to strike the coast later at the first convenient moment in a high latitude.

To overcome the lack of storage capacity, we proposed to raise the decks of the schooners by the thirteen inches which their waist permitted, and thus to secure additional space below deck: this allowed for a hold at the bow for general cargo and one at the stern for food supplies. Finally, in order to make good the resultant loss of free-board, we proposed to fit them with bulwarks, three inches thick and two feet high.

The viceroy, under whose immediate orders we were for the duration of this commission, approved this suggestion, and the work was taken in hand immediately on 2 January, ways being found to overcome the difficulty presented by the lack of means for effecting the most necessary repairs. Although there was only one carpenter and one caulker in the schooners, and these both of the third class, and although there were no other tools than the few belonging to the vessels, we hoped to receive help in our need from the royal frigate *San Andrés*, proceeding from Manila, which was then in the harbour under the command of the lieutenant of frigates Don Joaquin Berenguer de Marquina. As, however, his carpenters and caulkers were engaged on very important work on his own ship, they could not be employed on the schooners during the months of January and February. Consequently, the only workmen who could assist our two men were the few ordinary carpenters of the country and some Filipinos of the crew of the frigate *San Andrés*. We undertook to make good the deficiency by our own continuous help in the work, enduring every day the excessive heat of the sun in that unhealthy climate. Despite everything, the inadequate means at our disposal made the work which had been undertaken very difficult, and at every turn we encountered new obstacles.

The commandant of the department of San Blas, engaged in preparing various ships at the time when the schooners set out, had been unable to see that they came in the state which we asked, and so they were without wood, oakum, pitch, tools, and necessary workmen, which presented continual difficulties in the way of executing any work which might have necessarily to be undertaken. Men were sent ashore to cut wood and to prepare the necessary planks; the three sharp saws which we could find in Acapulco were brought into service, and the work on the schooners made progress. As for the supply of the necessary piping, in order that it might be secured with all possible speed, and as it was vain to seek for what was needed in the local stores or in the royal warehouses, the commander of the frigate of Manila, in view of the urgency of the orders of the viceroy, gave every assistance which his own circumstances permitted him to render. The means at his disposal were not equal to those which would have been found in other royal ships, for the commander of the vessel employed and equipped by the government for the direct trade between Manila and Acapulco for the benefit of the islands is directly subordinate to the Captain-General of the Philippines, and on his return from a voyage has to submit to a residencia held by an official of that audiencia. Hence, even when he had any of the things which were asked from him, it was necessary to give him a guarantee that they were indispensable, as they could be obtained in no other way.

The schooners had brought from San Blas supplies of food for six months, reckoning their complement as thirteen for each vessel. As, however, the timbers of the ships were thin, and the holds afforded no more protection than such as is given by the cabins of large vessels, the bread immediately went mouldy in the holds, while as a result of the slight seas encountered after leaving port, the partition between the two holds was broken so that the supplies were only fit to throw away. But the dried vegetables were of the best quality and the schooners carried means for providing in every imaginable way against any illness which might occur on board, even if the vessel did not carry any one competent to treat those who fell sick. For this reason, it was essential for us to give special attention to the holds, and when they had been made watertight, a coat of pitch was laid over them; they were then covered with tow and protected with some sheets of tin. The result was that we had two roomy larders, able to contain sixty quintals of bread each, instead of thirty-six as before, and in such state that the important supplies which they were to contain would be in no danger.

The schooners had come from San Blas with a complement which was half-way between that usual for schooners and that usual for brigantines. We found that this was unsuitable for the purpose for which they were to be employed, and therefore changed it, giving to the *Sutil* the exact complement of a schooner and to the *Mexicana* that of a brigantine.

Don Joseph Manuel de Alava, colonel of the regiment of Puebla de los Angeles, who was acting as governor and commandant of the castle in Acapulco, aided in fitting out the schooners with all such supplies as could be drawn from the warehouses of the place, providing us especially with the requisite number of muskets, pistols and sabres. The two vessels had arrived with no more than half the required supply of these arms, and even such as there were, in very bad condition, since the work to be done by the department at the time when the schooners sailed had been greatly in excess of the means at its disposal. The colonel also provided us with a leach, who was taken from those who were under sentence of transportation to the Philippines in the frigate *San Andrés*, and to this he added such books of domestic medicine as could be collected and given to us. The viceroy had aided our equipment with indefatigable energy and zeal for the good service of the king, qualities which he always displayed in the government of those vast dominions. He supplied us with money and issued orders and provisions, that we might be enabled to put the schooners in the best possible condition for the performance and discharge of our commission. We were thus provided with as many remedies against scurvy as were thought necessary, with as many kinds of articles of barter and of presents for the Indians as we thought fitting, and with such astronomical and mathematical instruments as New Spain could provide. This is the smallest debt which we owed to him; of greater value was the fact that he communicated his instructions to the governing bodies to give us assistance in terms which left us free to select the means which we should arrange for those instructions to be carried out as circumstances might allow.

On 7 March, the frigate *San Andrés* set sail for Manila with a fair wind, and the schooners remained making ready for sea and embarking supplies with a view to sailing on the next day.

We append a summary account of the condition in which these vessels set out on their voyage.

Schooner *Sutil*.	Schooner *Mexicana*.
Don Dionisio Galiano, commander of the expedition.	Don Cayetano Valdés, commander.
Don Secundino Salamanca, lieutenant of frigates.	Don Juan Vernaci, lieutenant of frigates.
	Don Joseph Cordero, cartographer.
Seventeen members of the crew.	Seventeen members of the crew.

Dimensions and Armament of Each Vessel

	Feet.	Inches.
Keel	46	10
Length over all	50	3
Beam	13	10
Draught astern	6	2
Draught forward	5	8

A swivel-gun mounted on a trestle.
Four small pieces of ordnance.
Eighteen muskets.
Twenty-four pistols.
Eighteen sabres.

The corresponding fuses and munitions; food and water for a hundred days; and various utensils and articles of copper, iron and other materials for presenting and distributing to the Indians.

Astronomical and Mathematical Instruments carried in the Two Vessels

A quadrant.
A pendulum.
Two achromatic spyglasses.
A telescope.
An azimuth compass.

A chronometer.
A marine clock.
Two barometers.
Four thermometers.
An endiometer.

CHAPTER II

Voyage from Acapulco to Nootka Sound.—The schooners go down to 12° north, owing to light winds and their slowness on the bowline.—The Mexicana loses her mainmast.—While she is being repaired, she falls away towards the shore and the voyage is delayed.—The winds favour the schooners and they arrive at Nootka.

FOR the whole morning of 8 March we waited for the wind, spending the time in storing away the goods which we had taken on board and longing for the moment when we could set sail, since that would mark the beginning of rest from the many fatigues which we had endured in that harbour. The wind did not rise until half-past one in the afternoon, and the schooners immediately weighed anchor. As the breeze was from the west, they fell away to starboard, and thereby revealed already their poor sailing qualities, and how soon it would be necessary to shorten sail. At sunset, they were two leagues outside the entrance to the harbour.

The winds continued to be light from west-south-west to west-north-west, and the schooners hauled to the wind in order to clear from the coast and to get the wind blowing from the south. Down to the eighteenth they lost latitude, falling away to 12° north, without gaining more than to 48° west. The winds had been regular, but sailing on the bowline in the best conditions they never made more than three miles an hour, although they shipped seas right over them, and the leeway was considerable.

From the eighteenth, the wind changed to the north, and an attempt was made to sheer a quarter to it, efforts being made to enable the ships to sail their best by every means which art could suggest, and sail being crowded on until the decks were almost always under water. Although the wind was not generally strong, it was fresh from the north and north-east. We still could not reach the latitude of Acapulco until the twenty-ninth, when we had an advantage of 15° on that parallel. Comparing our voyage up to this point with that of the corvettes in the previous year, we found that we required twice the time to accomplish the same distance with winds not less favourable. This day we had the misfortune to have our nautical barometer injured, it having been tied to the rigging for want of any more suitable place.

On the thirty-first, position was taken by the sun and moon, and this showed the degree of trust which we could place in the clocks, the longitude being found to be within a quarter of a degree from that which they showed. This was a matter for satisfaction, since owing to the leeway resulting from the bad steering of the schooners, it was impossible to rely on dead reckoning for the certain and secure determination of our course.

It was not until 5 April that the winds began to veer from the northeast to the east, our position being then 20° 40′ north and 21° 30′ west. For the next two days there were variable northerly breezes until the eleventh, when it changed again to the east, continuing to veer in this way for two days, when we first had a south-east wind. This raised our hopes, which had fallen low since we still found ourselves in 26° 4′ west and 27° 30′ east, and that we had therefore made very slow progress, partly because the winds had been lighter than is usually the case and partly because of the sailing qualities of the ships, to which reference has already been made.

On the fourteenth, we again took our position by the moon, and found that it agreed with our position by the clocks within half a degree. This day we navigated under full sail in the hope of making good the distance lost on our voyage, but at two o'clock in the afternoon, the *Mexicana* broke her mainmast at six feet and a half from the deck. This sad accident ruined our hopes of reaching Nootka in the short time which was essential if we were to have opportunity for caulking the vessels, for receiving the food supplies sent there for us from San Blas, and for undertaking survey work, availing ourselves of the whole spring.

As soon as the *Mexicana* was dismasted in this way, the *Sutil* hauled to the wind with lowered sails, her commander giving orders to pass the *Mexicana* in order that no worse misfortune than the dismasting might occur. Galiano steered such a course as he could and as seemed advisable, sending word that he would proceed under his foresail until the wind should fall and allow the carpenter to make good the damage done. Valdés replied that he would steer for Nootka, and that as soon as he arrived there he would secure the new mast needed for the continuation of the voyage.

The wind blew from the south with a very rough sea, and in the night veered to the west, coming in violent gusts and giving promise of foul weather. The *Mexicana* ran before it, with much sail set, that the vessel might be well under control, so that the work needed to secure the remains of the mainmast might be done. For this purpose shears were made from the oars of the schooner, and at the cost of great danger and labour, such as can hardly be realised, day broke to find the pole secured and all in the best possible condition for meeting any storm and for laying to, for the continuing of the voyage.

Three days later, the wind veered from west to south-west. The heavy seas in this latter period prevented the launching of the boat. The *Mexicana* continued to navigate ten points to the wind with the help of her mainmast. The sea eventually calmed, and the carpenter went to the *Mexicana* and continued the work of making some base upon which the mainmast could be fixed. A temporary mast was at last set up and next day its yard was fixed, being passed across from the *Sutil*, and at six o'clock on the morning of the twenty-first, that schooner was ready to continue her voyage. The accident of losing the mast produced no other unfortunate result than that of changing the course, obliging the schooners to abandon the direct route which they had intended to follow, and to fall away towards the coast, keeping along it at a distance of fifty-three leagues. If the wind should blow strongly from the west to the north-west, we were thus exposed to the danger of experiencing great delay in arriving at Nootka. For this reason an attempt was made to gain longitude with a course north-west 8° west whenever the wind allowed, but the wind was not sufficiently favourable to enable us to pursue this course without interruption. Until the twenty-seventh it varied from west to west-south-west, and the schooners continually hauled to the wind; but the current, which ran towards the coast with the strength of a mile an hour, according to the clocks, brought the vessels to within twenty leagues of it at 41° 48′ north.

From this time until the second of May we experienced favourable winds from the third and fourth quarters, and advantage was taken of this to bear away from the shore, taking care in so doing not to lose latitude. Those pilots who are well acquainted with the coast advise that a course should be steered for 28° west of San Blas or 33° 30′ west of Acapulco, and not nearer the coast, regarding the prevailing wind as north-west. Nevertheless we observed much variation in it, which caused us to vary the course according as circumstances made it advisable. It was the intensity of our longing which caused us to realise the error of those pilots.

On the second of May, at 43° north and 29° 30′ west the winds varied from south-west to south. On the fourth they veered to the fourth quarter, but were favourable and light, so that it was possible to haul to them. On the seventh, at 46° north and 30° west the wind changed to south, and carried us a considerable distance towards Nootka, although it was

MACUÍNA

necessary to tack in order to keep to the course which we were steering obliquely for that harbour, calculating the direction and distance by the chronometers checked by observations of the moon.

On 12 May, at dawn, we were in sight of Cape Frondoso. All day and night we navigated along its parallel with a clear sky and fresh wind, and at dawn on the thirteenth found ourselves in sight of the harbour. On our arrival there came out to meet us in a canoe the chief or tais Macuina, accompanied by his relatives and friends. We presented him with an axe, four knives, and some pieces of hardware. He immediately recognised Valdés, Vernaci, and Salamanca who had been at Nootka in the previous year, and greeted them with a show of great satisfaction, following the schooners to their anchorage.

We felt secure to the fact that the coast is clear and that the rocks near it are visible, and so went very near the islands by which the harbour is formed. The *Sutil* grounded in the shallow water near its south point, but freed herself in a few minutes without suffering any damage. Both schooners were assisted by towing from the boats and launches which had come out to aid us, and we came to anchor at two o'clock in the afternoon.

It must not be concluded from this accident to the *Sutil* that the entrance of that harbour is dangerous. The rocks which there are in the creek between Point Macuina and the entrance to Nootka are very visible, and can be passed without special care at a distance of two cables. The islands of San Rafael and San Miguel, which close the mouth of the creek and form the harbour, reduce the width of the entrance to less than a cable, but may be passed at a pistol shot's distance. Both islands are very lofty, and are rounded. On the island of San Miguel there is a battery well placed for the defence of the harbour and of vessels anchored in it.

It does not seem to be out of place to mention that to make an anchorage with the winds from the west, it is necessary to keep very close to the shore of these islands, taking the precautions which have been mentioned, and on coming to the entrance of the harbour to luff, furling all sail. Then if the wind be moderately fresh and the vessel one of somewhat fine lines, with the way which is on her she will come to the best anchorage, which lies to the south-west of the island, and even without these conditions it will always be possible to find anchorage of a suitable kind. It is also possible to anchor outside the points, where there is considerable depth of water, suitable for anchoring even at a short distance from the mouth of the harbour.

CHAPTER III

Ships in the harbour of Nootka.—Refitting of the schooners.—The corvette *Aransazu* arrives.—Good relations with the Indians.—Arrival of the French frigate *Flavia*.—Astronomical and physical observations.

WE found anchored and dismantled in the harbour the frigate *Concepcion*, under the command of Don Francisco Eliza, lieutenant of the navy, who resided on land as commandant of a provisional settlement which we had maintained there since the beginning of 1790. There were also there the war frigate *Santa Gertrudis*, under command of Don Alonso de Torres, captain in the navy, and the brigantine *Activa*.

The governor of the settlement and of the ships was Don Juan de la Bodega y Quadra, captain of the navy, who had come in the frigate *Gertrudis*, with the object of carrying out the convention concluded between our court and that of England in 1789.

This commander had orders from the viceroy of New Spain that he should assist the schooners in whatever way was necessary, but the scanty resources at his disposal and his many duties rendered him unable to attend to the work of refitting them with that activity which we wished. Our needs were limited to changing the principal ropes, which were constantly breaking owing to their bad quality; to providing for each schooner a supply of good tackle, five inches thick, to serve as a mooring-rope; to making a mainmast and mizzen for the *Mexicana*; to lengthening her crossjack and topsail yards; to providing her with a launch, which was done by shortening a boat belonging to the corvette *Concepcion*; to lengthening the boom of the *Sutil*, to repairing her boat and for getting the two schooners supplies of tow, pitch and tar, and other necessities which were wanting; to increasing the complement of the *Sutil* by adding two marines, a gunner, a caulker, and a sailor in place of one who was ill, and that of the *Mexicana* by adding a carpenter and three marines.

On the thirteenth the frigate *Aransazu* arrived, coming from San Blas, to make certain surveys to the north of Nootka.

While we were in this harbour, we saw with special pleasure the close friendship which existed between the Spaniards and the Indians. Macuina, influenced by the gifts and good treatment which he had received from the commandant Quadra, had come to live very near the ships. He ate every day from his table, and although not at it, yet very near, using a fork and knife like the most cultured European, allowing his servants to wait on him, and delighting all with his festive behaviour. He drank wine with pleasure, and in order that his mind might not be fogged left others to determine the amount which he should drink of that which he called "Spanish water." He was generally accompanied by his brother, Quatlaza-pé, towards whom he showed the greatest affection. There were also accustomed to eat in the chamber certain relatives and vassals of his, and for these last there was placed every day a plate of kidney beans, as they preferred eating these to anything else. Macuina was endowed with remarkable ability and quickness of intelligence, and knew very well his rights as a sovereign. He complained greatly of the conduct of the foreign vessels which traded on the coast, on account of certain wrongs which, he said, had been done to his people. He denied that he had ceded Nootka Sound to the English lieutenant, Meares, and only confessed that he had allowed him to establish himself there, repeating continually that he had made over to the king of Spain the harbour and so much of its shores as belonged to him with all the products of those shores.

Quicomasia invited us, on 20 May, to a bay which was by his settlement, which was in the interior at a place which we called Malvinas. This tais is the same as he who in 1791, when the corvettes were there, called himself Quicsioconuc, and as a result of having married a daughter of a tais of the Ñuchimases he had changed his name, taking another, as we understood, of more importance. We were never able to understand in what the difference consisted, but he was very vain of his alliance, which he valued as a fact which gave him an advantage over Macuina. He said that he was tais of Nootka and a Nuchima tais, and accordingly superior to that chief. A dance took place, some pilots providing the music. Quicomasia appeared in fancy dress, sometimes with feathers, sometimes representing various animals, among which he imitated the bear to perfection. Sometimes he went on all fours, and acted as if he were being attacked by a hunter. After this amazing performance, he placed himself at some distance in front of our people, and naming each one of us individually in a loud voice, caused us to be given otter skins. Another day he came to visit us on the schooners. We gave presents to him, as we had been already warned that it was for this reason that he had come; he told us that he received our gifts as presents, not as articles of barter or exchange, since taises did not engage in commerce, but made gifts and received them. In order to rouse us to make him presents of greater value, he proceeded to explain to us how entirely superior he was to Macuina.

This vaunting each above the other is the main topic of conversation among the taises. Tiupananulg, putting two of his fingers together, always told us that there was as little difference between him and Macuina as between those two fingers: we did not observe that in their intercourse with one another either showed the other the least respect, and that the one did not display much satisfaction at the preference shown to the other by the commandant Quadra. He always plumed himself on the services which he had rendered with his great canoe to the Spanish ships, and of his continual gifts, but in this respect Macuina was not his inferior, since when he noticed that Eliza was short of supplies, before the arrival of ships from San Blas, he ordered his Mischimis to provide our settlement with fish, and they did so punctually, without seeking to receive any kind of return. Despite this, Tiupananulg persevered in coming once a week to the commandant Quadra, almost always bringing some game; he ate near the table on the opposite side from Macuina; he spoke little, and his manner was dull, but good-natured.

On the twenty-second, two Indian canoes arrived from Claucuad. In the principal canoe came a brother of Wicananish to visit Macuina, of whom it is said that he was a relative. All regarded him as the sovereign of the shore from Buena Esperanza to the point of Arrecifes, and of all the channels running inland. Thus, while we did not see any clear evidence of respect in Quicomasia, and still less in Tiupananulg, it seems that he should be regarded as their overlord and they as his vassals. The Indians of the canoes from Claucuad were very fat, and in appearance compared very favourably with the Notkeños. Among them the tais was distinguished by his bizarre appearance. The Indians were well provided with muskets and powder, since Wicananish had acquired many weapons by bartering his skins with the Europeans, whose desire of gain had led them to fall into the imprudence of giving assistance to the formation of a respectable power in the dominions of that tais. While such ships as have visited that district could report that the laws of hospitality had not been broken and that they had always received the best treatment and reception from the Indians of these coasts, it is with the proviso that nevertheless it is always necessary to be observant of behaviour and actions. For, while the taises are able to maintain the best possible order, yet at times a misunderstanding, resulting from ignorance of the language, might produce the most fatal consequences. We gave presents to the Indians from Claucuad, and informed them that if the weather were favourable we would accede to the request made to us to visit their chief, but we did not meet their great wish, which was that we should give them some powder.

On the twenty-sixth, a ship was sighted, whereupon the flag was hoisted on our fort and the existence of the harbour thus revealed: the boat of the frigate *Gertrudis* went out to pilot the visitor to her entrance. She was the French frigate *Flavia*, of some five hundred tons, and her captain, M. Magon, flew the new national flag, which we saw for the first time. The object of the *Flavia* was to trade for skins along this coast and then to proceed to Asia to sell them, and to gain information concerning the unfortunate expedition of Count de la Perouse, in order, if possible, in any event to render assistance. It seemed to us that this purpose was very secondary, when the course which the *Flavia* was following was taken into consideration.

During our stay at Nootka, the weather was very varied: the winds still did not cease to blow from the south, bringing rain and cloud, as if the winter were not yet quite ended. On this account it was impossible to observe the eclipse of the chief moon of Jupiter, which the tables announced for the night of the sixteenth, and although this occurred again on the night of the eighteenth, complete confidence could not be placed in this observation, since the sun was only six degrees below the horizon at the time when it occurred, which was at 8° 30′ 20″ true time. On comparison with the tables, it was found that the longitude of Nootka was 120° 30′ 15″ west of Cadiz. We kept a look-out for the repetition of the occurrence on the twenty-fifth, but rainy weather prevented the observation from being made; it would have been of interest for settling exactly the longitude of this harbour. In the previous year it had also been impossible to make the observation completely from the corvettes, which had had only means of making lunar observations. The latitude of the sound had continued to be given as 49° 36′ 16″ north, and we found it only 4″ farther north. On the twenty-eighth, an eclipse of the second moon of Jupiter was observed, and gave 19′ farther west than as ascertained on the eighteenth. The clocks were carefully examined, but the barometers could not be used as their tubes had been broken. The thermometer kept at a height of 14 to 17, and the endiometer gave the following results:

	First Observation.	Second.
Air in the hall of the commandant's house	60	53
Open air	54	52
Air in the hall of the hospital	—	52

The first observation was made on the twenty-eighth, when the sky was clouded, the wind slight from west-south-west and the thermometer at 16. The second was made on the twenty-ninth, when the sky was in the same state, the wind north and the thermometer at 17.

CHAPTER IV

*The schooners leave Nootka, and are forced back into harbour by the bad weather.
—An American vessel insults the Indians of the Buena Esperanza Inlet.—
Instances showing the good character of Macuina.—The schooners again
leave and arrive at Nuñez Gaona Sound at the entrance of Juan de Fuca,
where they encounter the frigate* Princesa.

THE schooners being ready, we weighed anchor at four o'clock in the morning, sailing with a land breeze to the north, although it was light and the weather fair. The narrowness of the harbour and the need for rounding the point of Arrecifes necessitated the departure being made at the first dawn of day, in order to be free of the harbour while the wind remained off the land. The launches of the vessels, taking soundings, guided us until we were outside the harbour. We took the smaller vessels on board, and made all sail, steering south-west to south in order to round the point mentioned, and to proceed on our course with a west wind, from which direction the wind always blows between ten and twelve o'clock in the morning.

We were not far out when the wind changed from east to south and we continued to beat west-south-west. At half-past ten in the morning we turned east-south-east, relying on the tide, which would assist us until two in the afternoon, in the hope that with a slight increase in the wind we might be able to round the said point and its reef, although the former lay right ahead.

The weather then began to grow threatening; the sky was covered with thick cloud and the land with mist, and the wind, which had changed to south-east, began to rise. On this account, at half-past four in the afternoon we made towards the harbour, with the intention of returning to it if the weather did not clear, since during the days before our setting out we had observed that it was very variable. However, the mist grew thicker, it began to rain without ceasing and the south-easterly wind to grow stronger. These circumstances determined us to make our way to our last anchorage, which we successfully regained at eight o'clock in the evening.

The night which followed was cruel; there was a high wind, and it rained heavily, so that we were thankful indeed that we had made so safe a return to harbour, since, if we had not done so, we should have had a night as critical as any sailor could experience.

On the following day the same weather continued, and Macuina, who came to be with us according to his custom, told us in his own language, accompanying his words with gestures, which he was able to make expressive, that we had not selected a fit time for setting out and that the selection of a time might safely be left to his care. We accepted his offer, reflecting that the Indians who live by fishing, in which they employ vessels as frail as are their canoes, must necessarily observe weather signs closely, and be able to foretell the weather as accurately as our best fishermen. But Macuina signified that his prayers to Cuautle gave him more confidence than his own knowledge, and in the very house of the commandant he intoned these prayers with the greatest devotion. We were unable to understand more than the words "Cuautle-Clus-nas," that is, "God, good weather." As his intoning and his grimaces moved us to laughter, Macuina showed that he was annoyed, and it was necessary in order to pacify him to explain that his actions made us laugh because they were very strange to us. The Mischimis heard him with the greatest devotion; they signed their disapproval of us because we did not imitate him, and gave us to understand that we could rest assured of the good result of the prayers of their tais, as they had often experienced their good effect.

This day there came a canoe from outside the harbour with various natives asking help from the commandant Don Juan de la Bodega against a ship which was in the Buena Esperanza Inlet and had there attacked an Indian settlement, killing seven men and wounding others, and robbing the rest of the otter skins which they had. They brought one wounded man for the surgeon to heal, and Macuina interceded with the commandant that care should be taken of this man and that he should proceed to chastise the aggressors. As far as could be understood the ship was the American frigate *Columbia*, Captain Gray, whom the Indians indicated by making signs that he was one-eyed, which we knew to be a characteristic of that captain. They said that the natives had not wished to engage in bartering skins with the Europeans, and that they had used force to make them do so.

The exchange value of copper had fallen as a result of the competition of European ships, and the merchant captain who came to trade, not knowing this, overestimated the value of his cargo as being that which it had been in the past. When he began to trade, he found that the Indians had raised the price of the skins and that, at the rate of exchange which they demanded, increasing loss would result for him; forgetting the principles of equity and believing that his actions could not be investigated, he availed himself of force for his own advantage. To this cause must be assigned the wrong done to the Indians at Buena Esperanza Inlet, and if the governments from whose jurisdiction the ships which engage in trade on these coasts set out do not impose rigorous penalties on captains who fail to observe the laws of right conduct, offering rewards to such as keep strictly to them, they will incur the greatest blame. It may be regarded as certain that the Indians of Nootka are incapable of attacking any ship which arrives on their coast, since they all have the greatest respect for the arms of the Old World. Further, a certain rectitude and dignity is observable in the conduct of the chiefs, and this inspires esteem and confidence. We cannot do less than quote two instances which occurred during our stay in Nootka Sound and which prove that our security was justified. One day we saw Macuina enter the house of the settlement with an expression which betrayed his mental unrest. "I have sentenced to death," he said, "one of my Mischimis for having committed the wrong of having intercourse with a girl of nine years in the seclusion of the woods; they are now inflicting the punishment, and I have come here in order not to suffer the pain of hearing his laments." When he decided to return to his encampment, he told our officers that if they wished to assist the unhappy family of the criminal, they might give him bread or anything which might be useful. How worthy of admiration it is to see in the midst of this small number of wretched men, in the first stages of civilisation, living in a corner of the world, a chief in whom are united the qualities of a legislator, judge and father of his subjects.

Another day a criminal, sentenced to death by the same chief, sought the protection of Don Juan de la Bodega, throwing himself at his feet. The commandant offered to do what he could for him, and when the chief came to visit him, asked pardon for the supplicant. "It is granted," said the chief, "but he must not return to associate with my people; let him remain where he is; make him cut his hair and dress as do your people, and if you do not forget that which I am doing, for the sake of it I ask that some time you will grant the same pardon for one of these people."

On the fourth, the sky having cleared, Macuina did not fail to warn us that the weather was now settled and that we could make our departure. In the evening we went to visit him at the house which he had near the settlement; he received us with the greatest of pleasure, and showing much friendliness, presented salted salmon to us, offered us whale, smiling on learning that it was repugnant to us, but being satisfied that

Don Cayetano Valdés tasted it. After spending some time with him, we returned on board, meeting on the way many canoes, which were already setting out to fish, proof of the confidence which the natives had that the weather would be fair.

We were glad during these days to be able to replace a marine, whom we were forced to leave behind sick, by a naval gunner, who was an excellent hunter. Luis Galvez, the leach in the *Aransazu*, also asked to come; the crew had great confidence in his skill. Accordingly the leach of the *Sutil* was transferred to the *Mexicana*, which was short of a man to complete her complement of twenty-four, with which it was determined that the schooners should proceed to their survey work.

At half-past two in the morning warning was given to the launches, and at three o'clock we were outside the point. The wind was fairly fresh from the north-north-west; the weather was clear and appeared to be sufficiently settled for us to make the direct course so as to pass in to the reef at the end of Arrecifes Point. The wind fell directly we were outside the channel which forms the entrance to Nootka Sound, and we lay becalmed until eleven o'clock in the morning, when a sea-breeze rose from the west-north-west. It freshened in the evening and we ran before it under all sail, making seven miles by the log, which is the greatest speed which we observed in the schooners. From five o'clock to seven the wind dropped, and at nightfall we were sixteen miles west and ten north of the entrance of Nootka Sound, and five miles from the small islet which we had made our objective.

We were bound, in view of the circumstances, to direct our attention to hastening the examination of the entry of Juan de Fuca, and for this reason we did not wait to investigate the points on the coast which we sighted. We only ran under some to place them and to rectify the map which the officials and pilots of the department of San Blas had made and which we found to be little exact.

We continued to proceed under all sail during the night, steering east, five degrees south, with a fresh wind from west-south-west. The clearness of the night, which after the tenth was greater owing to the moon, seemed to assure us that we were secure from danger. At two o'clock the wind died away almost completely, and morning broke to find us half a league to the south-east of the east point of Nitimar, and in sight of the mouth of the strait or sound of Juan de Fuca.

The calm continued until eleven o'clock, but the currents caused us to drift about a league to a point within the entrance of the strait; we noticed that the currents caused a number of small waves, although their strength did not seem to be sufficient to do so. As soon as we were near the strait, we observed on the coast to the north, from which we were half a league distant, clumps of seaweed which sailors know by the name of "sargasso." Taking soundings in the choppy water, we found thirty-two fathoms depth. A sailor who is used to navigating on this coast knows that the plant in question is generally a sign of shallow water, as are small waves of this kind, being formed by the currents meeting some obstacle; we have verified this on many occasions by our own experience.

At eleven o'clock the wind blew from the south-west, and we steered east-south-east in order to cross the mouth of the strait. We saw several canoes which were fishing and some came alongside. They told us that they were from Nitimar and invited us to go there to trade for skins. We secured a large fish in exchange for a knife, but one of the Indians would not barter a necklace of glass beads which he was wearing. Many of them accepted a nail in exchange for the spike which they wore through the cartillage of the lower part of the nose. The appearance of these men was unlike that of the inhabitants of Nootka; their heads were of normal shape, their eyes small and close together; they were shaggy eyebrowed and seemed to be cheerful and friendly. They prized copper highly and cared little for knives.

At four in the afternoon, we sighted the harbour of Nuñez Gaona, and shortly afterwards saw a corvette at anchor; we concluded that she must be the *Princesa*, belonging to the department of San Blas. We pursued our course in order to coast along the west shore of the harbour, and presently there arrived Don Salvador Fidalgo, lieutenant of the navy, commander of the corvette, and confirmed us in the idea that the coast west of the harbour was shoaly, as the appearance of the sargasso suggested. We fell away somewhat to windward and after tacking for a time eventually came to anchor at half-past six in the evening very near the *Princesa*.

CHAPTER V

Don Salvador Fidalgo proposes to form a settlement at Nuñez Gaona, similar to that at Nootka.—Account of the district and harbour.—Good relations with the Indians.—The chiefs Taisoun and Tetacus visit the schooners.—Astronomical observations.—Tetacus accepts the invitations to make a voyage into the strait in the schooners.—They set out from Nuñez Gaona.—Best method of navigating into the strait.—Friendly care of Tetacus.—The schooners reach the harbour of Córdoba.—Restlessness of Tetacus until a canoe arrives with his wife, Maria.—Visit to the natives.—Character of Tetacus.

It was a month since the corvette *Princesa* had arrived from San Blas, and her commander, Don Salvador Fidalgo, was awaiting orders from Don Juan de la Bodega to decide whether a station should be formed or the harbour abandoned; it was necessary to discuss the matter with the English commissioners who were expected at Nootka according to the convention concluded between our court and that of England in 1789. Fidalgo had selected and caused to be prepared a site with the idea of making a garden, and the plants which the commandant had brought from San Blas had been already planted there. He had built an enclosure for cattle, cows, sheep, rams and goats; near there was a barrack where a guard was stationed to attend to the care and good order of everything, and preparations went to the extent of making ready to winter there if necessary.

The land, although generally of the same character in soil and products, seems to be kinder than that of Nootka, and the climate pleasanter and more healthy. The country is cut up by small streams and surrounded by woods and lofty mountains. The harbour is exposed to the north-west winds and even to those from the south-west, and it is violently swept by winds which come through an opening in the mountains in this direction. Rocks run out a considerable distance from the beach, and the surf breaks upon them with such violence that it is difficult and dangerous to make a landing.

The Indians were very friendly, being flattered and given presents by Fidalgo in the same manner in which the people at Nootka were treated by Don Juan de la Bodega. Although their language is very different, they understand Nuqueño, and their customs are apparently the same as those of the natives of that island. They are taller and more robust than the people of Nootka and are better built; their faces are better proportioned and they are fairer, so much so that we saw two women who might be described as white. The ordinary clothes of the men is a woollen cloak and a cape of skins, either otter or bear, but some appeared with coats of blue cloth, buttoned from top to bottom; these they had received from European ships which had come there to trade for skins. The dress of the women is less modest than that of the women of Nootka; their clothing is limited to a cape of skins, joined at the neck, and they have no underclothing except a bandage tied round their waist, from which hangs a very wide fringe of pine needles or other plants so as to cover them down to the knees. They uncovered their nakedness without any embarrassment, and with little enough shame, in their canoes and on land. They wear many bracelets of copper or of stag's horn, necklaces of shells, whalebone, copper or glass beads. In the same manner they decorate their noses and ears with such things hanging from them, the ends of which they keep always sharp; they paint themselves red and black; they use grease to make their hair shiny, and they give just as much attention to their extravagant adornment as do the women of Nootka.

For the shells of Monterey and for iron, these natives care little; they do not even place much value on copper. Old clothes is the best article of barter among them; as is the case with other savages, the moment for exchange is that at which they first see the thing, and then there is no cape, cloak or wide coat which cannot be bartered easily. We did not see that they had any great stock of skins or other articles of exchange or barter.

During our stay at this harbour, we found the natives affable, confiding and lively. On the first day we let them know that only the chiefs would be allowed to come on board, and from that time we did not relax this rule or cease to keep careful watch. This was the more necessary since we had noticed their thievish inclination and how they were constantly able to hide the thing stolen before we saw it in their hands. A small boy offered to bring women for us, and we inferred from this that these women were slaves, as are the boys which are offered for sale in the same way as at Nootka.

Fidalgo did not rely with entire confidence on the natives, taking care, as was right, to guard against some fatal accident, owing to his knowledge of the attacks which these Indians had made on ships which had appeared on their coast. He had accordingly ordered that a cannon should be fired at sunset, as a sign to them that after that they must not come near the corvette or the station until daybreak; he immediately found the greatest readiness to obey this regulation among those to whom it applied. On the same account he had not been ready to give them arms, and he even asked us not to give them knives.

The chief, Taisoun, came on board the *Sutil* soon after she had anchored, making a present of sardines before he did so. This custom we had never observed at Nootka, nor could it be kept up, considering the poverty of those savages. We made return to him in the shape of shells, glass beads and some small copper pans. He saw over the ships and retired, well satisfied with the treatment which he had received from us.

Tetacus, one of the principal chiefs of the harbour, and who, according to information which was borne out by his conduct, was one of those most attached to the Spaniards, also came on board and asked with the greatest eagerness to be allowed to look over the ships. Permission was given to him, and he examined them with a curiosity which we had not otherwise found among these Indians. Afterwards, on board the *Sutil*, he said that it was his wife who was in the canoe which remained by the shore; she was called Maria, a name which would have seemed to be some corruption or due to defective pronunciation, had it not been that careful attention was paid to the manner in which Tetacus pronounced it. When we were told this we pressed her to come on board, and she excused herself with an air of doubt or uncertainty. We gave Tetacus to understand that we had no other motive in urging her to come on board than to do a politeness to his wife, and that if she were prepared to condescend to do so, she could rest assured that she would not receive the slightest insult or impertinence. Her husband then ordered her to come on board and she obeyed, stretching out her hand to be helped up. They remained on board with the greatest confidence; we gave them presents of some trifles, and they left us well pleased with the thought that this tais had sufficient trust in us to be, with his favourite wife, alone and unarmed on board a ship which he had only just seen and among people of whom he had no sufficient knowledge to form so good an opinion of them.

Our work in this harbour was limited to making a chart of it, observing its latitude with sextants at obtuse angles or by the sun, and its longitude by marine clocks. We reached the conclusion that the difference between Nootka and Juan de Fuca Strait had been wrongly determined by abstract calculation, there being an exaggeration of 57′; the lay of the coast was thus greatly modified. The thermometer was steady at sixteen to nineteen degrees, and the endiometer gave the following results, which showed the superiority of the air of this place over that of Nootka in point of healthiness.

Open air	65 parts.
Second test	67 parts.
Air within the wood	63 parts.
Air of the cattle shelter, on the ground	53 parts.
Second test	53 parts.

This was at the time of little wind; the sky clear, and the thermometer at nineteen degrees. The weather had been continuously fine; on the morning of the eighth, we were ready to set sail, having received from Fidalgo a sharp saw, some tow and medicine, and we only awaited the wind to set out.

Tetacus came to the schooner *Mexicana* at eight o'clock, and, leaving his wife Maria in the canoe, came on board, greeting the officers with the greatest pleasure. When they presented him with a cup of chocolate, he gave proof of the affection which he had for his wife, since, having found at the first sips which he took that the taste was pleasant, he immediately moistened a piece of bread with it and was insistent that she should share in the treat. After having paid a visit of some while to the officers, he asked leave to go, and told Valdés that he must leave that morning for his settlement, which lay farther within the strait. Valdés invited him to make a voyage in the schooner, and Tetacus did not refuse the offer, but showed that he was pleased by it. He at once took a piece of dried fish, which he had in the canoe to support him on his journey, and hung it from the rigging of the schooner, and ordered his wife to continue her voyage. Shortly afterwards there came to the coast a canoe, in which there was another of his wives, an older woman and not so good looking as Maria, and as Maria prepared to obey the wish of her husband Tetacus, so the second tried to show that she was more devoted to him than was Maria by displaying the fear aroused in her by the confidence with which Tetacus had trusted himself to us. With earnest prayers, accompanied by the most tender weeping, she urged him to leave the strangers and to make the voyage in his canoe. Tetacus attempted to calm the fears of this woman, but she reiterated her cries and nothing availed to console her. He therefore made up his mind to give way to her, and explained to Valdés that he must leave us and accompany her. The commander realised, however, that if he were to meet Maria in the inner part of the strait, or any of those who knew him and who believed that he was going in the *Mexicana*, they would suspect

Selma lo grabó.

TETACÚ

30

Selma lo grabó.

MARIA

31

that some injury had been done to him, if they did not see him on board. In such an event we should have been in danger of coming into conflict with some nations, to remain on friendly terms with which we had spared no effort; although it had at the same time been necessary to inspire respect for our arms, the only means by which it was possible to hold in check the natives of these coasts, who had on more than one occasion attacked the ships of navigators who attempted to explore the district. He made Tetacus understand this, and Tetacus laboured to persuade his wife by the same arguments, but failed to attain the same result, and since he did not wish to appear to be indifferent to the signs of tender affection which she had given, he made signs to Valdés and Vernaci that they should seize him and lead him to the cabin, not giving him freedom to go away. These discussions occupied some time, and the woman, despairing of attaining her object, went off with renewed lamentations, having been given some glass beads. We found much to admire in the conduct of this chief. Master of great wealth, and holder of power over many leagues in that district, alone, without arms, in a vessel the management and safety of which were unknown to him, he trusted himself to some strangers whom he had seen on the previous day for the first time. He did this without showing the least uneasiness, suspicion, or regret for his decision to do so; on the contrary, he gave evidence of the greatest satisfaction during the whole time that he was with us. He watched and asked questions with a degree of interest which made it clear that his chief reason for accepting the offer which had been made to him of undertaking this voyage was to acquire knowledge of our organisation and of the way in which the ship was managed. He paid careful attention to the working of the vessel; he watched the handling of the cables, and inquired their names, and few things escaped his notice. He was careful not to weary us, interposing some apology in his questions, and supplying us with details of the customs of his country and giving us the names of things which he believed might be of interest to us.

Although the naval ensign Don Manuel Quimper had surveyed as far as Quadra harbour, and the naval lieutenant Don Francisco Eliza as far as the Channel of Our Lady of Rosario, in previous years, no survey had been made of the entries of Caamaño and Flon, of Gaston Bay, the channel of Floridablanca, and the entries of Carmelo and Mazaredo. According to information received from the Indians, the entry of Caamaño ran far inland, but its depth was insufficient for the passage of anything except canoes; that of Flon was of much less importance. It was held to be certain that Gaston Bay was blocked, and the most interesting exploration was held to be that of Floridablanca Channel, which, as depicted in the chart which had been made of these channels, had two entrances, formed by an island lying in its centre, which was afterwards found by our survey to be the peninsula of Cepeda and Lingara. The channel, as had been understood from the Indians, ran far inland, and there had been found among those of that district some bracelets of copper engraved with great skill.

Being possessed of such information, we decided to begin by completing the examination of Gaston Bay, and to proceed to the survey of Floridablanca Sound, leaving the examination of Caamaño and Flon as being of less importance, and as being most properly to be undertaken in the event, which we believed to be very probable, of our being compelled to turn back. The trend of the channel of Caamaño was to the south, and the possibility that it led to that of Ezera at about 46° 14′ north was another consideration which persuaded us to adopt this plan.

At twelve o'clock the wind blew from south-east; the fair weather showed us that in the channel the prevailing wind was west. At half-past twelve we set sail, and steered to pass through the small channel which is to the east of the islet at the mouth, which we did successfully. This channel is very narrow owing to the reefs which run out from the points which form it, and so it should only be used in cases of necessity or when some decided advantage is offered by its use. It appeared to us that it would serve our voyage well, since it was our intention to follow the south coast of the strait, as this was supplied with many excellent anchorages. As in the case of the northern shore, the land is mountainous; while, however, the hills there are low and rounded, containing areas which are lovely and covered with grass and pines, a country suitable for cultivation, the south shores are lofty and the peaks of its mountains appeared to be covered with snow. As soon as we were out of the channel we knew that the route to be followed in order to penetrate into the sound was that along the north coast, since on the course which we intended to follow there was the most perfect calm. When we saw the degree of motion in the water caused by the wind, it was necessary to launch the boat and to use the oars in order to meet it. This manœuvre seemed to be good on our passenger, Tetacus, who, when he saw that it was difficult for us, owing to the calm, to reach the point where there was wind, had been troubled. He stretched out his arm and began to play with his fingers, doubling now one, now all of them, opening two, raising one and leaving it so for a while, and there was in all his actions something which indicated to us that he was praying mentally.

When we had reached the wind, we steered towards the north coast, navigating north-north-east and approaching the shore from the east until we were proceeding close to it. At eleven o'clock at night we coasted along it at scarcely a league's distance, and followed this course with a fresh west-north-west wind, the weather being fine and pleasant.

Morning found us near Point Moreno de la Vega, and we rounded it so as to pass between it and the small islands which were near it; this route was suggested by Tetacus and was one which those who had navigated this strait strongly advised. Having made this position, the wind veered and we continued our course with light breezes from west to south all the morning. Several small canoes came out from the shore near this point, and we gave some glass beads to the Indians in three of them which came alongside. They understood the Nuqueño language, and one of the sailors in the *Sutil* knew that one of those natives had in the previous year been among the most active in attacking the launch of the packet-boat *San Carlos*. We steered to the harbour of Córdoba, where Tetacus indicated that he must stop, and to which he gave the name Chachimutu-pusas. Tetacus had slept soundly all night, never feeling any less freedom and trust; his bearing gave continual evidence of his quick understanding. He recognised on the map the configuration of the strait and islands which had been discovered, and told us the names which he gave to them. When he had doubled Point Moreno de la Vega, he informed us that we should take in water there, as it was good and plentiful, because, when that point had been passed, springs were scarce and the water ill tasting. He ate with appetite whatever we gave him, copying all our actions, which he always watched carefully. He remembered the names of all the English and Spanish captains who had visited the coast of the mainland and the archipelagos of Claucaud and Nootka, and further informed us that there were two large ships within the strait.

When we came near Eliza anchorage, three canoes, with four or five Indians in each, approached the *Mexicana*, but they would not come alongside. The natives were dressed in cloaks of wool, and they brought other new sheepskins which they were prepared to exchange for a piece of copper. On this occasion an action of Tetacus was noticed which displayed his generosity. He took off four bracelets of copper, very well made, which he was wearing, and handed them to Vernaci, and told him to use them to get the cloaks which the Indians were wearing. The officer wished to barter two bracelets for one of them, and when the owners would not agree to his proposal, but wished to receive four, the tais said that he should give them all. This, however, was not done, Vernaci knowing that Tetacus, being pleased with the good treatment which he had received from Valdés and with a leathern jerkin and a hat which had been presented to him, was ready to make this sacrifice in order to give the cloak as a return. The natives who came in these canoes were well formed, and their cheek-bones were so low and flat that their appearance was very like that of an European. One boy was specially remarked, who, if he had been met in Spain, would have been taken for a Spanish boy. They presented Valdés with some fruit, like figs in shape, black, and of a floury character, with a salt taste. They were given in return some strings of glass beads, which they at once hung about themselves with much pleasure.

At eleven o'clock in the morning, we proceeded to enter the harbour of Córdoba and anchored in six fathoms of water, the bottom being sandy and in the south part of the anchorage. The canoe containing the wives of Tetacus had not arrived, and he was in a state of great uneasiness. He took the glass and searched every part of the sea, giving more and more proof of the affection which he had for his wife Maria. He was in this state until the canoe arrived at one o'clock; the two wives were together in it. He entered it, embraced them and returned on board, where he ate with us. Our insistence on this occasion that one of the wives should come on board the schooners did not avail, doubtless on account of her advanced age, which prevented her from overcoming the fear resulting from the fact that she was already somewhat frail and that she was faint-hearted. Tetacus bade us good-bye with the greatest cordiality, and went ashore with the women.

We observed that the canoe had a large carved eagle at its bow, as we had also seen in the case of other war canoes. All these Indians seem to have some kind of fear or veneration for the effigy of this bird, as have also the natives of California, because, as they say, they owe it special gratitude for having pulled an Indian out of a pit. Tetacus had taken a pencil which was on a table, and, among other drawings which he made on a piece of paper, he drew with accuracy an eagle in the act of flying. It had a very large head and two horns on it; he represented it as having thrust its talons into a whale, and he assured us that he had seen a bird of this kind swoop down suddenly from a height to the sea near his house, fasten it on a whale and bear it away. Valdés retorted that he must have been sleeping when he believed that he had seen such an extraordinary thing, and he assured us that he was as wide awake as now when he was telling the story. Despite our ignorance of their religious beliefs, of which it is impossible to gain knowledge, this indicates the great part which is played by fables in the creed of these peoples; so much may be judged from the fact that one who passed among the taises as very enlightened had the most vivid imagination in these matters.

In the evening we went ashore to visit the village of Tetacus, where there were some fifty Indians. They stretched cloaks for us to sit on, crowded all round us, and presented us with some of the food which they had. Tetacus showed the greatest friendliness to his guests, interspersing his conversation with continual embraces. He showed us all the courtesies in his power, with simple goodwill, and we returned on board very pleased. During the night there was the most complete quiet in the harbour. We kept watch to guard against any unfortunate accident, since, although we were well assured of the friendship of Tetacus, we did not as yet know the degree of respect and obedience which he received from his people. We afterwards learned that he was one of the most feared of all the chiefs who live on these shores, and that he had won the greatest respect and authority among them, on account of his bravery, ability and character.

Various Words in the Language spoken on the Southern Branch of Fuca Sound, and their Equivalents

Ihaac	Water.
Alii	There.
Taciu-hamach	The sky.
Guinda	Monterey shell.
Zumocianelo	Rope.
Licitle	To make a cut.
Lluisac	Stars.
Lacuec	Smoke.
Taquisamach	Tongue.
Clejacle	To weep.
Glajuahashitle	Moon.
Guvachas	Mountains.
Suushuc	To swim.
Aya-mas	I do not understand.
Ucutap	Bird.
Claquetum	Ship's mast.
Glisapic	Ship's sail.
Upar-daquia	Sunset.
Zujucitle	To wound.
Daquia	The sun.
Sisabache	Flat land.
Guisimut	Cultivated land.
Tuishi	North.

VARIOUS WORDS IN THE LANGUAGE SPOKEN ON THE SOUTHERN BRANCH OF FUCA SOUND, AND THEIR EQUIVALENTS—*continued*

Cuasini	North-east.
Balegsti	West.
Dados	To hear.
Pipi	Ear.
Suayuk	The bird like an eagle which Tetacus depicted.

NAMES GIVEN BY THE NATIVES TO VARIOUS POINTS ON JUAN DE FUCA SOUND

Harbour of Nuñez Gaona	Quinicamet.
The island at Martinez Point	Chani.
Settlement of Roxas	Isjuat.
River Canel	Chismit.
Harbour of Davila	Ucuas.
Harbour of Quadra	Chlayamat.
Island of Carrasco	Chachanecuk.
Channel of Caamaño	Quechinas.
Floridablanca Sound	Sasamat.
Harbour of Revillagigedo	Machimusat.
River Cuetsa	Sisachis.

CHAPTER VI

Account of the harbour of Córdoba.—The schooners leave it and anchor near the south-east point of the island of San Juan.—Observation taken of the first moon of Jupiter.—A canoe comes alongside.—The schooners weigh anchor and proceed to Guemes Channel.—Inhabitants of the shores of this channel.—They survey Gaston Bay.—They anchor in it.—They ground and get off without injury.—They set sail and enter the channel of Pacheco. —The two vessels are parted.—The schooners proceed by night by the creek of Garzon, where they find evidence that ships have anchored.—They attempt to enter the channel of Floridablanca between points San Rafael and Cepeda, and fail to find anchorage owing to the shallowness of the water.

THE harbour of Córdoba is beautiful and affords good shelter to ships, but water is scarce in it, as Tetacus told us and as we verified from our own observation. The land is very diversified, of no great elevation, and it appeared from the land round it that there is little depth of earth over the rock. It is certainly fertile, covered with trees and plants, which are almost the same in character as those of Nootka, wild roses being more plentiful. Birds were also rather more plentiful; there were special species of gulls, ducks, kingfishers and other birds. It was in this harbour that the schooner *Saturnina* was obliged to open fire in order to protect the launch of the packet-boat *San Carlos* against the canoes of the natives; the launch had approached them and they made determined efforts to take her.

As the weather was unsuitable for us to make any determination of the latitude and longitude of the harbour by day, we set out at three in the morning as the tide was coming in. From eight o'clock in the morning we were able to avail ourselves of the land breeze, which was favourable from the south-south-west. We steered to the middle of the channel in order to be able to get the full force of the wind and to make our way to the island of Bonilla which serves to mark the course well. We passed some shallows where the currents ran very strongly, and on reaching the islands so steered as to leave them to starboard. At five o'clock in the evening, when the wind tended to fall, we made the south-east point of the island of San Juan, in order to anchor on its easterly shore, which we did at nine o'clock in the evening.

The principal reason for coming to anchor here was in order to take an observation of the first moon of Jupiter, which we were especially anxious to do in order to fix the longitude of Nootka, and to calculate the bearing of other points to it by means of chronometers. We therefore landed with the instruments, and having observed the transit of the moon in peace, we returned on board without finding any sign of inhabitants. The result of this observation was checked by reference and gave the harbour of Santa Cruz at Nootka as 120° 26′ 00″ west of Cadiz, and as we had every confidence in the accuracy of this observation, we were able to use it as a basis for the determination of the longitude of other places by their difference from that of this point.

When we came to anchor, the tide was at the turn; we took an observation of its force and found that it was never more than a mile and a half, towards the south-south-east, an hour, up to three and a half, and that it turned at this hour. The water rose eight or nine feet.

At seven o'clock in the morning, there was a light breeze from the south-south-east. We set sail with it in order to avail ourselves of the tide so long as it favoured us: the weather was cloudy and visibility was only a mile. We tacked in order to reach the east coast, not only in order to run along it and so not to miss the entrance of the channel of Guemes, which lies between the island of that name and the coast, but also in order to make the islands which lie in the middle of the channel in which we were, and towards which the current carried us very rapidly. In proportion as we drew nearer to the middle of the channel, the wind freshened and blew more strongly. We accomplished the distance which brought us to the east coast, and coasted the two islands of Morros with the aid of the land breeze which blew from the south from eight in the morning, driving away the clouds. We arrived at the south-west point of the channel of Guemes, and entering it steered at first towards its centre in order to get out of the calm near the shore. Within the channel, however, the wind changed its direction and we approached the south coast in order to escape the force of the current, which was contrary to us; in this we were so successful that, although the wind was variable, we made three and a half miles an hour. The voyage was very pleasant, owing to the well-wooded coasts. To the north, at the point where there is a breach near the entrance, we saw a settlement near the north-west point, and this on further examination appeared to consist of two large houses; many Indians ran down to the beach, embarked in a canoe and made their way towards the schooners, following them as quickly as they could and with as much skill as the most experienced sailor. In this canoe there came alongside, in perfect confidence, an old man and four young men of agreeable appearance, and they presented us with mulberries, taking some of those which they carried in a large shell three or four inches in diameter, and which hid that which they did not offer to us. We gave them each a metal button, and they made more gifts of the same kind in order to receive something in exchange, not being lavish in their offerings but bargaining, seeing that for each thing which they presented we gave them a string of beads or a piece of sea biscuit. They also gave us cockleshells, of the kind which sailors call verdignoes, fastened to a piece of the bark of a tree, and others of a different kind fixed in small pieces of wood. We collected enough of these, and there was also taken from them a dogskin cloak decorated with feathers and a tanned skin. Meanwhile, we were following the south shore of the channel in six fathoms, with a sandy bottom, as far as the south-east point, and from there we changed our course, making for the point which lay to the north-east, close to which we passed, in order to go along the shore of the island of Guemes, and by way of that island and of Tres Hermanos, we made our way into the bay of Gaston.

After we had doubled the north-east point, we found ourselves becalmed, and it was necessary to make use of our oars in order to reach the desired point, as some light winds from the west-south-west were contrary to us. As soon as we had passed the islands, however, the wind veered to west and we tacked to port in order to make Punta de Solano. The heat greatly troubled us, since, although the thermometer in the shade was not high, in the sun it registered twenty-nine and a half degrees and would have risen farther had it not been that we were meeting the direction of the wind.

At five o'clock the wind changed to south and we altered our course, entering the bay of Gaston, part of which we coasted, although it was not entirely reconnoitred. We steered towards its end, in order to discover whether there was a channel. The wind freshened, and favoured by it we were satisfied by nightfall that there was nothing more than a small river flowing into the end of the bay. The shore, which was low-lying and marshy, since the bay lies between two heights, was at some distance from the navigable channel; the depth of the channel was six to seven fathoms, with a rocky bottom, and we proposed to make our way farther into the bay when we found that we were in five fathoms with a hard, chalky bottom. On this account it was preferable to anchor, having observed the direction which the wind was likely to be in during the whole night. The position was a good one for anchoring and leaving the more detailed examination of the bay until the following morning. We furled all sail and the helmsman of the *Sutil* reported four fathoms. The anchor was dropped, but when thirty yards of cable had been run out, it was found that the schooner was in two and a half fathoms.

The commander at once gave orders to take soundings from the poop and poop rails; at two cables' distance, two fathoms were found, and it was discovered that the anchor was in three fathoms. This error on the part of the helmsman placed us in a very difficult situation. The night was a time of great anxiety, during the whole of which the tide was running out so that at dawn we found ourselves in a fathom and a half. We had seen lights to the south-east on the mountain of Caremlo, and at times heard some rumblings, which were undoubted signs that in that direction there were volcanoes in violent eruption. The *Mexicana* had anchored two cables farther to the west and in a half fathom's less depth; the wind, which had fallen during the night, became very strong from the south-south-east in the morning, and the sea began to come over the poop. She at once paid out a cable to her long-boat and at the same time set sail in order to keep her head to the wind. Meanwhile the *Sutil* had dragged her anchor, and found herself in two fathoms of water; she had taken her boat on board in order to make sail when we learned that the *Mexicana* had grounded. The boat was therefore launched again and sent to aid her. This schooner had had the misfortune to foul the small anchor which had been passed with the cable to her long boat, and was thus very exposed to the danger of capsizing, her crew using the oars to keep her straight and to avoid this disaster. The *Sutil* also fouled her anchor as soon as she set sail, and as soon as she had moved, she found herself in hardly six feet of water. Proper means being taken, however, at the end of an hour both vessels were afloat again.

The ships at once proceeded to set sail in order to continue their voyage, and at half-past eight in the morning they were sailing with a fresh wind from south-south-east in order to get out of the bay of Gaston, without inquiring whether there was any channel, although within the bay many waves were seen.

After much manœuvring, at four in the afternoon they reached the south and west points of the bay of Gaston, and entered the channel of Pacheco. They steered through the middle of it, the wind falling somewhat, and following the direction of the channel as soon as the ships entered it. After coming out of the channel, in the creek of Lara, we saw two small vessels, one by her rig a small coasting vessel, and the other square-rigged. They were going along the coast northwards, and we had no doubt that they were the two English vessels which were in the strait according to the information which we had received from our friend

Tetacus. We went on without changing our course, intending to navigate under light sail all night, and to reach Point San Rafael by dawn so as to be at the mouth of Floridablanca at the beginning of the morning. We proposed to enter it in order to make an immediate examination, since, as has been said, we had reason to think that it would be full of interest. Between ten and twelve at night, we passed the creek of Garzon, and saw lights in it, which indicated to us that the vessels to which the smaller vessels were attached were lying at anchor there.

The wind, which was fresh all night, enabled us to make the distance almost to Point San Rafael by one o'clock. We tacked with sails trimmed in order to keep out to sea from it, and at two in the morning were beyond it, finding ourselves in six fathoms. We continued to bear out to sea and the depth grew constantly less until it was five fathoms, with a sandy bottom. In this situation it seemed to be well to come to anchor in order not to waste the night searching for the entrance, as it would have been unwise to attempt an entry without some fuller knowledge. We anchored, and with the first dawn we found that we were in mid-channel, in the entry between Point San Rafael and the east point of the peninsula of Cepeda.

CHAPTER VII

In the morning the schooners reach this closed passage.—Visit from the English brigantine *Chatham*, whose commander, on behalf of Captain George Vancouver, requests that our expedition should join with his.—The wind does not allow this.—Departure of the *Chatham*.—The schooners attempt to penetrate into the channel of Floridablanca by Point Langara, and are prevented by the current.—They anchor, and leave on the following morning.—They are in danger in Porlier Entry.—They arrive at Descanso Creek.—Difference of character between the Indians of these two shores revealed by the events which occurred.

At daybreak the boat went to take soundings in the direction of the channel of Floridablanca, with instructions to return as soon as it found shallow water. At five in the morning we set sail, following the boat, under light canvas, but we had gone no more than half a mile with a fresh south-south-east breeze when we were in three fathoms. We changed our course, approaching nearer to the coast, and found the water still shallower; we reached the coast of the peninsula and the depth increased to four fathoms, on which account we headed towards the channel. But in a short while we found three fathoms, and the boat which we had sent out coming alongside, also contributed to confirm the impression that it was impossible to enter the channel of Floridablanca between the east point of the peninsula of Cepeda and point San Rafael. On the other side, we saw no opening at the end of the creek, and only found that it ended in low land, marshy and full of trees. The boat, which reached a point where there was hardly a fathom of water, confirmed us in this view.

Since one of the two mouths of the channel of Floridablanca as depicted in the map made in the previous year had been found to be barred, the impression which we had already formed on the earlier expedition was strengthened. We hoped, however, from the entrance which was in view that the channel ran many leagues inland, and so were anxious to try the entrance lying north of Point Langara.

We tacked in order to attain this object by rounding the peninsula of Cepeda, and were so doing when at seven in the morning we sighted a square-rigged vessel which came out from the direction in which we had believed that the two ships were anchored. Soon afterwards we saw that she was flying the English flag, upon which we showed our own colours. She proceeded to follow us, and we saw that she was a brigantine. Having come up to the stern of the *Sutil* and saluted us, her commandant asked us if he might come on board; we replied by declaring the pleasure which it would give us if he did so, and presently an English officer came on board the *Sutil*. We continued our course along the land, and informed him of the small depth of water in that direction.

The brigantine was the *Chatham*, commanded by Lieutenant William Robert Broughton, R.N. He was with the corvette *Discovery*, and under the orders of Captain George Vancouver. These vessels had left England on 1 April 1791 on a voyage of discovery. They had been to New Holland, New Zealand, and the islands of Tahiti and the Sandwich Islands, and had afterwards followed the north-west coast of America from 45° north to the Fuca Strait. They had entered that strait on 5 May, and spent some time in charting it. We told the officer of our departure from Acapulco, our arrival at Nootka and our leaving that harbour, and that we had left there Don Juan de la Bodega, captain of the navy, who was awaiting the English vessels, which were to go there. The English officer informed us that his object was to suggest to us on behalf of Captain George Vancouver that he should supply us with any help that we needed, and to invite us to the anchorage where he was, where we should find abundant water, which was not very generally the case along the strait. We thanked him and offered him our help, promising to join his expedition if the wind permitted it, but as it was contrary for reaching his anchorage and favourable for continuing on our course, we showed him that we could not for the moment accept the offers of Captain Vancouver. We supplied Broughton with such information as we had so far gained concerning the navigation of the channel, and of the results of the examination made by the Spaniards in previous years, and told him that we had information concerning his anchorage and of the sound which there was near there. We also supplied him with an account of the purpose and condition of our vessels, telling him that it was our intention to examine these channels and to fix their positions exactly. The English officer answered us with equal frankness, saying that they were carrying a clock of Arnold and another of Kendal, that the brigantine was of one hundred and fifty tons, that she drew fourteen feet, and the corvette was of three hundred tons, with a draught of fifteen.

After these matters had been concluded, the officer returned to his ship, and made towards the west, presently rounding Point Cepeda. We continued on our course without being able to follow him until two in the afternoon, when we reached and followed the coast towards Point Langara, in order to anchor near it, to spend the night there and, when it was over, to enter the channel of Floridablanca on the next day.

The wind continued to be very favourable, from the direction of the land along which we were coasting, and although we navigated at two full miles from it in sixteen fathoms with a sandy bottom, we suddenly found ourselves in two fathoms, on which account we turned out to sea until we were in ten fathoms and then continued on our course. At five in the afternoon we noticed ahead a line where the water changed colour, there being many breakers there towards the land. We came up to this point, finding no bottom at twenty fathoms, and afterwards when we had proceeded for half a mile, we saw that the current was carrying us away from the coast very rapidly, bearing us towards the west and to mid-channel. We put out our oars, endeavouring with them to counteract the current, but as the efforts of the sailors proved to be vain, as they were very wearied with the exertions of the previous days, it was decided to cross to the south coast in search of an anchorage where we could pass the night. We steered so as to cut at right angles the line of the broken water, the wind being gentle and from the east, and when we had done this, we steered for the shore, near which we arrived at nightfall. We went along it until we had found fifteen fathoms with a sandy bottom at two successive soundings, and then dropped anchor. The launch and boat were ordered to take soundings and to determine the distance which we were from the beach, and it was found to be three cables' distance, with deep water and a clean bottom everywhere, so that there was almost four fathoms of water close inshore, while to make our security the greater, it was found that at a cable from our anchorage there was a depth of twenty fathoms. To this secure mooring-place we gave the name The Anchorage.

The wind had fallen, but after midnight it changed to north-east and we kept careful watch. The current was not noticeable, and was not so all night. The sky remained cloudy with frequent showers, and it was so at daybreak.

In the morning Vernaci went in the launch to search for a good anchorage to the north-west, from which we believed that it would be possible to make Porlier Entry, from which we did not think that we were very far distant. Our position was between the two points which are to south-east of these straits, at an equal distance from each.

The wind began to blow more strongly from the north-west, and our position would give cause for anxiety if it blew strongly from that quarter. At half-past eight in the morning the launch, which had set out at half-past four, was not in sight, and its delay began to cause us some concern. In a short while, however, we sighted it, and it came alongside without having been able to find a suitable anchorage in the two leagues for which it had proceeded.

As the weather did not allow the schooners to make along the north coast, it was determined to proceed with them in search of the desired anchorage. We set sail at nine in the morning, hoping to find Porlier Entry. We reached it at midday and easily entered it without waiting to send the launch forward to investigate it, since although the wind, which we had had fresh from east-north-east, left us when we were under the shelter of the point at the entrance, the waves carried us farther on, as they ran strongly in that direction.

When we had made the entry, we found an archipelago of many low, small islands, and discovered that the channel divided into two chief mouths, one lying to the south-east and the other to the west. It was at once resolved to follow the former, in order to have always the help of the wind to get out of it if necessary. But when we had lost the shelter of the coast, the *Mexicana* experienced a sudden gust of wind from the direction of the channel, which was so strong that she was in danger of capsizing. We immediately realised the danger in which we should be among these islands, the channels between which we did not know and which we had no interest in exploring. The wind, forced to pass through the narrow space which divided two mountains, blew with extreme violence; the currents were strong and were driven to take different directions owing to the numerous islands which barred their way, and as we saw no beach, it was clear that there would be no suitable anchorage. We could not pass far into this entry, since it was likely that much time would be spent in doing so to the prejudice of our main exploration of the mainland, and it thus seemed to be wise to put out to sea without delay.

But the task of getting out of these channels was not so easy as we had hoped. The currents had gained such strength that we could not counteract them with our oars, the wind being light and soft. The result was that we had to spend two hours of great exertion and danger in order to get out of the channel. The *Mexicana* succeeded in passing to windward of the islet at the entrance and very near the end of its reef in four fathoms, the rocks being visible at the bottom. The *Sutil*, however, which began to adopt the same course, preferred to change it in order to pass through the narrow channel which the islet forms with the coast, and she accomplished this easily.

On these channels there are several native settlements which have been abandoned, and there is one inhabited on the west coast of the entrance. From this five canoes came out with ten old men and nineteen young men, all very robust and of good appearance. They reached the schooners and presented us with mulberries and nuts, and received in exchange buttons and necklaces. When it was known to them that we were in need of fresh water, they went to their settlement and presently brought us some casks full of it.

Being free from the danger in which we had been, we followed the coast with the design of finding a good anchorage. We steered directly to Point Gaviola, and not touching it, we went on to the entries of Wintuysen, being aided by a fresh easterly wind, with which the sky became clear. When we had reached the point to the east of the said mouths and passed between them and the islet, after doubling the point mentioned, we saw lying near the shore two canoes watching the movements of the schooners. When we came opposite to them, they approached us with considerable caution. To win their confidence and friendship, we gave those who came in them such proofs as we could of our intentions, throwing to their canoes some strings of beads, but we could not persuade them to come close. We continued along the coast with the same object, until we finally found an anchorage a full mile from the point, and, as it appeared to be suitable, we steered for it. We named this anchorage Descanso Creek, on account of the need which we had for it and our delight at finding it then. It was now five days since we had entered the strait, and in them we had not merely rectified but had also increased the knowledge which had been gained in previous years, a fact which consoled us for our fatigue and labour, no less than did the hope of continuing to carry out our remaining tasks with equal success. With this aim we set to work to replenish our stock of wood and water, and to take the other measures which our situation demanded, with all possible zeal.

When the task of making the schooners fast was finished, we landed on the beach which was at the end of the bay, and proposed to go into the wood to look for fresh water. But we had not gone far when we saw some natives of the land, who made signs to us that we should not go farther, and others who ran off, as we supposed, to warn their women. We did them the pleasure of going back, giving them to understand the purpose of our coming. Thereupon two of them led us to two very poor springs which were on the coast to the east of the harbour, about two cables farther on than our anchorage. In one of these there were three basins made of rounded stones, and this confirmed our impression of the scarcity of water along these coasts. With this information we made our way to the beach, and found six Indians who were presenting sardines to our sailors; they were given in return necklaces and other signs of friendship, but it was not possible so to inspire them with complete confidence.

On this day there collected near the schooners thirty-nine canoes, two or three Indians being in each one of them. We found a noticeable difference between their appearance and that of the other natives whom we had seen in the strait, but that which made the greatest impression on us was the fact that many of them were blind in one eye, which was covered with a short skin. They had pointed beards and very bushy eyebrows. Their clothes were generally no more than a cloak of rough wool and well woven, joined by two clasps at the shoulders and not hanging down below the knees. Here and there one was wearing a skin, that of the man who seemed to be the chief meriting special attention; he wore under it another cloak of fine wool, a hat with an ornament like a shortened cone, five tin bracelets on the right wrist and one of copper round his neck, this last being very similar to that which we had seen worn by an Indian at 60° north in the previous year. Some wore hats, and many were painted with ochre. They were smiling and seemed to be docile, and if they were not stupid, they were at least not quick-witted. Their language was entirely different from that of Nootka, and they talked more loudly and with a guttural enunciation, so that the task of understanding them seemed to us to be more difficult.

They offered to barter with us large quantities of sardines dried in the air and smoked, and arms which were merely arrows, some with a point of stone or cockle-shell very well made, and others with bone worked into a saw, pieces of whalebone and bows of moderate size made of very strong and knotted wood. They also offered new cloaks, which we afterwards gathered were made of dog's hair, both because we could discover no difference in their texture from that of dog's hair and because in their settlements there were a large number of these animals, most of which had been shorn. They are of moderate size, apparently similar to English-bred dogs, very long-haired and generally white; among other characteristics which distinguish them from those of Europe is their manner of barking, which is no more than a miserable yelping.

We were extremely sorry to find that despite all the efforts which we made and the continual evidence of friendliness which we showed to these Indians, we were unable to win their confidence. They were still always restless and suspicious; at the least movement they were alarmed, and our intercourse with them was thus frequently interrupted.

They valued the necklaces and the Monterey shells; from the inside of the latter they made ornaments. They showed more appreciation of rough pieces of iron than of such as was fashioned into knives or nails, perhaps because they could make use of it to point their arrows, for their harpoons and for other purposes.

There is a remarkable difference of character between the natives on the Porlier Entry and the Wintuysen entries, despite the short distance which separates them. The former are confiding and friendly; the latter suspicious and unpleasant. Perhaps, however, the same difference may be observed between other nations equally near to each other and in a higher state of civilisation. If among peoples who live under similar laws the manner of their education suffices to produce this result, it can hardly be regarded as strange that it does so among these tribes, who would appear to be independent of one another and to have no constant intercourse with one another, as we observed from the fact that their canoes do not proceed for more than a certain distance from their settlements. These reflections should be present in the minds of navigators, warning them never to rely upon the savages on these coasts, despite the fact that they may have found some neighbouring tribes to be humane and friendly.

We spent the night resting, our company being divided into four watches and the necessary sentinels being posted, that the rest, trusting to the watchfulness, might repose in peace. The night was calm, and throughout its duration there was no disturbance at the anchorage.

Part of the following day was employed in arranging and setting in order our records of observations, charts and calculations, and the notes made on all matters, which, having been jotted down on board ship in the midst of toil and labour required to be systematically expanded in order that they might be in good order and not convey a confused idea of the information gained. We also replenished our supply of water, twenty barrels of which could be filled in a day in that district.

The savages did not overcome their suspicion despite all the efforts which we made to make them understand our peaceful intentions—no insistence and no attentions sufficed to induce the chief to come on board the *Sutil*, and all the canoes kept close together and made for the shore from the schooner with much commotion. At the same time, bartering went on without any disturbance and they continued to provide us with fish until the afternoon, when, discovering that the boat of the *Sutil* was being launched in order to go to the shore, all who were near that vessel became alarmed and made off, not daring to come near the schooner for the rest of the day. There afterwards appeared at the anchorage two canoes which attracted our attention on account of the hideous appearance of the four Indians who were in them; they were all pimply and presented a most unpleasant sight. They showed us their arms and gave us to understand that they were not afraid of us; we replied by making signs of friendship and goodwill, and they retired, rather satisfied with their defiance than with our intentions.

In no other part of the coast had we noticed so ingenious a method of fishing as that which we observed among these Indians. They carried in each canoe a harpoon of cockle-shell very well made, fixed on the end of a fairly large stick, at the other end of which was a small fork. They also carried a piece of wood shaped like a cone, at the middle of the base of which were fixed some thin and roughened pieces of bark like feathers, the whole having the appearance of a wing. They hid the fork among these pieces of bark, and when they saw a fish at a great distance under water, they enticed it into the cone with great gentleness, the point of the cone being underneath and close to the head of the fish. They then withdrew the fork and pulled the cone to the surface of the water with a speed which prevented the fish from noticing it. The prey was in this way brought to the surface of the water, and an Indian, who was ready with the stick and had the harpoon in hand, struck it, generally with such accuracy that it was seldom merely wounded.

On the fifteenth and sixteenth, rain had been almost continuous, but on the seventeenth we had the most delightful springlike weather. Under a clear sky there was displayed to us an attractive country; the green, of varying tints and shining, of some woods and meadows, and the majestic rush of the waters which fell from the heights at various points, entranced our senses, and was for us all the more pleasant because we had so recently passed through so many trials and labours. Wishing to profit from this for the refreshment of the crews and for the extension of our own knowledge, Salamanca landed with five men, carrying arms and laden with necklaces and trifles, in order to proceed to the place where the Indians had their settlements, to see whether they had been abandoned, as we inferred from the fact that armed canoes had gone out.

Salamanca found the land which he went to see covered with brambles and full of very straight pines; he saw the remains of the settlement which the Indians had abandoned, and then returned on board.

On the eighteenth, the boat put out again and continued the collection of water, and in the afternoon we went in the launch to examine the interior of the mouths of the Wintuysen and to discover the inner parts of the entrances seen on the previous day. The second of these, counting from our anchorage, is narrower than that of Descanso, but not so clear and not such a good mooring. We afterwards followed a channel which tended east-south-east, and which from its direction must lead to the archipelago which we had seen from the former point to the east of the harbour.

CHAPTER VIII

The schooners leave Descanso Creek.—They proceed along the north coast and anchor hurriedly on account of the shallows.—They set out again and reach the east of Point Langara.—Visit from the natives and arrangements for exploration.—The English vessels are sighted, and the junction of the expeditions is decided upon.—Explorations in the channel of Floridablanca.—The schooners leave.—They join with the English, and anchor near the Quema island.

Having taken the opportunity to advance our surveying and astronomical work, having revived the strength of the crews and replenished our stock of wood and water, we set out at five in the morning with the intention of examining the channel of Floridablanca. The weather was fair, and we felt now and then a slight soft breeze astern. As soon as we were outside the channel, we found that the wind freshened to east quarter north-east, and on this account we hauled to the wind with the bow to north quarter north-east in order that we might reach the entrance which we wished to examine. This task occupied all day, and when night fell we experienced a violent shock on the bow, which was the result of our having collided, owing to the carelessness of the watch, with a large tree which was floating on the surface of the water and which might have caused us great damage. We drew it to starboard with an anchor, and as we were doing so the boat which we were towing astern was in great peril.

At two o'clock we were very near some low-lying land, and not finding bottom at forty fathoms, unwisely kept by it, looking diligently for an anchorage. We knew from the reports of other voyagers and from our own experience, that there was often a change from great depth to shallows, and on this account it was preferable to pass the night standing by.

We continued to approach the shore until two o'clock: we hove to with the bow to north-north-west, having only the topsails set. At half-past three, with daybreak, we reached Point Langara and went along the coast, taking frequent soundings, but although at three o'clock we had not found bottom at forty fathoms, a quarter of an hour later we suddenly found ourselves in three fathoms. We tacked to the wind, which was fresh from the west, and finding that the water continued to become shallower, we anchored two and a half fathoms, realising that the currents were carrying us towards the coast.

From the south-west side of Point Langara, seven canoes came out and made their way towards the schooners; they were of moderate size and very like those which are used at the entrance of the channel. Each carried two or three Indians, who had taken off their cloaks and so were left entirely naked; one and another was wearing a hat, and most of them were painted in various colours. The appearance of these natives was better than that of the other Indians whom we had seen all along that channel; the shape of their faces was more perfect, and their physiognomy was like that of Europeans. Their muscles, although not very large, were better formed than those of the inhabitants of Nootka, and they were not so white, but the liveliness, grace and intelligence of these natives greatly impressed us. They exhibited a friendliness which surpassed that of the others, while at the same time they showed themselves to be of a warlike disposition. They were clearly provided with many excellent weapons, such as spears with iron points half a yard long, sheafs of arrows with points of the same metal and of stone, bows and machettes, which they held in high esteem, so that it was impossible to barter for them knives or Monterey shells. They had also in their canoes various chests, some being filled with harpoons of stone, arrow-heads, nets of grass and other implements useful for fishing. When they came alongside they at once presented us with a salmon without suggesting that they wished for any return, nor did they show any appreciation of the necklaces with which we repaid them. They accompanied us for some distance, and went away, leaving us wondering at the difference in the appearance, in the persons and in the character of the natives of this strait within a few leagues' distance.

Shortly after anchoring we found that the current was carrying us inshore, and suspecting that the water was shallower, we verified this by sounding. We took the precaution of setting sail and tacking to starboard with the bow south-west, and so the water grew progressively deeper until it was ten fathoms, and soon afterwards sixteen. We followed the same course until half-past seven in the morning, which found us with Point Langara to the north 3° east and we hove to, with the bow pointing north-north-west in order to come close to it.

From our anchorage the extreme north point of Point Langara was to the north 15° west, and the most salient point of the peninsula of Cepeda was to the south 49° east. This last is lofty, and so is the coast which stretches from it towards the south-east for the distance of half a mile, but from that point it is very low and marshy, and no rising ground appears up to the extreme end of the peninsula. In the previous year our officers from the department of San Blas had visited it. On proceeding some distance along this coast, and not noticing the lowest part of it, they had imagined that the lands immediately near Point Langara and the peninsula of Cepeda consisted of two islands lying in the mouth of the channel of Floridablanca, and so marked them in their map.

The coast of the continent lying between the channel of Guemes and the entrance of Mazaredo consists of low-lying land near the sea, but at a short distance inland it becomes mountainous, and the peaks are always covered with snow.

The mountains lying at the end of the channel of Floridablanca form a very narrow gorge, with the result that at a distance the marshy land between them cannot be seen, a fact which afforded a pleasant illusion to those who visited this district in search of a strait to the other sea.

At nine o'clock we saw four canoes coming from the direction of the south of Point Langara; three were of the same build as those which had been seen previously, the other was larger, and in her came two youths paddling, an old man of grave bearing who seemed to be a tais, and three other persons who accompanied him. We offered them necklaces, but they signed that they held them in low esteem. However, we secured a canoe in exchange for some small copper sheets, our intention being to use it for keeping up communication between the schooners when their boats were occupied in some reconnaissance. The old man came on board as soon as it was suggested to him, and showed frankness and confidence.

The wind freshened from the south-west and we ran before it towards Point Langara, south 65° east, sounding constantly with great care. At twelve, having made sure that there was enough water in the creek formed between the Point of Langara and the coast, we proceeded to go to anchor in it, at a place where we knew that there was sand. We went there to wait for the rising ride to assist us to pass through the channel when the depth allowed. Our plan was to send the launch and the long-boat to take soundings at two cables' distance, and to follow them in the schooners with all the care necessary in view of the variable wind; in this way we learned that the current in the part where we were anchored ran at four and a half miles an hour, and might therefore be supposed to be much stronger in the inner part of the channel. We were already in water which was almost fresh, and we saw floating on it large logs, which indications confirmed us in the idea that the bay which we called Floridablanca was the estuary of a considerable river.

The wind had almost entirely fallen away, and we made very slow progress; despite this, we took careful soundings at sixty fathoms, since, while we were unable to find bottom, we had learned from our own experience that we might suddenly be in very shallow water. In actual fact, we found bottom at twenty-five fathoms and directly afterwards at fifteen, and after manœuvring with the idea of anchoring, we let fall the anchor in ten fathoms, our anchorage lying with the most northerly point of Point Langara to the east 5° north.

In the afternoon there came near us two canoes with several natives, who regarded us with smiling faces and signs of confidence. Their language appeared to be very similar to that of those whom we had seen in the creek of Descanso, but their open character, their liveliness and cheerfulness were preferable. They repeated what was said to them with great ease. One came on board; he wished to have, and was given, a ribbon, with which he was much pleased, repeatedly thanking us for that with which he was adorned. The sailors sang the "Marlborough" and the Indians accompanied them, continuing the tune by themselves when our people had stopped. They sold us some bows, arrows, machettes and three small casks for the canoe, since those who had let us have the canoe had gone away without consenting to leave us these things. No one of the natives remained in sight in the evening, from which we felt sure that they did not come from the settlement which we saw near Point Langara. They had made many signs to us that we should proceed farther within the channel, giving us to understand that we should find food and abundance of water.

At the point at which we had anchored we found that the tide ran south-west with a force of half a mile, and this agreed with the information which we had concerning the speed of the current, although we supposed that there must be much variation in it, owing to the eddies and backwash caused by the direction of the channel.

At two in the early morning a large log was seen coming towards the bow of the *Sutil*, which was warded off with a pole and an oar; the current never had great force, since its speed was not two miles. At seven in the morning we saw a boat approaching, which we did not doubt came from the English vessels; it made its way to the *Sutil* and ran alongside her, there coming on board the commander of the expedition, Mr. Vancouver, his first lieutenant and a midshipman. Mr. Vancouver said that he had been engaged during the last two days in exploring various channels, and showed the maps on which figured the channels of Floridablanca, Carmelo and Mazaredo. We examined these papers with interest, and were surprised to see that the first of these channels only ran inland fourteen miles to the east; the second two united to form one and in a northernly direction, 10° east, extended to 49° 38′ north. Of the third pair, one of which to the east is narrow and the other to the west very wide, incline towards each other until they form one, and continue afterwards to 50° 10′ north in a northernly direction 25° east for two-thirds of the distance, and finally north 10° east. He had also examined the mouths of Caamaño, and these channels run inland with various ramifications as far as 47° 5′ north, one of them having a branch which runs north to join the channel of Flon. We exhibited the map which we had made of the part of the strait which we had examined, and after these reciprocal proofs of frankness, Mr. Vancouver pursued his suggestion for a union of the two expeditions. This proposal offered to us the advantage of achieving the examination of these channels in less time, their importance being already lessened by the limitation of the branches of Floridablanca and Carmelo, and also enabled us to take advantage of the excellent weather to navigate to the south in order to examine the entrance of Ezera and to rectify the chart of the coasts lying between Fuca and San Blas.

It was with this idea that we informed the English commander that our people would conduct him back if his own men were tired, at the same time letting him know that the schooners would leave if the wind were favourable, and that they would immediately direct their course to form a junction with his ships, hoping in this way to meet his wishes and to please him.

It was not possible for us immediately to carry out our intention owing to the calm, and in the state of inaction in which we found ourselves it seemed to be well to send the launch and the boat to examine for ourselves the channel of Floridablanca, the more so as from this no disadvantage could accrue, the commanding officers, Vernaci and Salamanca, having been instructed to rendezvous in the harbour in which the English were, since the schooners would set sail as soon as the wind proved to be favourable.

The Indians followed in good accord with our men, and so much so that when the canoe which we had bought from them came apart, one of them came on board and wished to direct its refitting, which he did to perfection.

On the twenty-fifth, the dawn was overcast, a light wind from the south-east, and although the boat and launch were not in sight, they appeared at half-past five and came alongside at six, having examined the channel east-west which the English had not shown on their map, and further, another which was on the north coast of the same, and which our friends had not seen.

Most of these channels presented an entirely novel aspect. Following the main line of the coast, several gorges are noticed, and if one proceeds into any one of them, an arm is found, generally tortuous, of moderate size, one or two miles broad, formed by the slopes of some rocky mountains, very lofty, cut almost straight, so that they look like a very high wall. In the middle of these channels, bottom cannot be found at eighty fathoms, and on taking soundings near the shore, the line could sometimes be allowed to run out without reaching the bottom. Any one who enters these channels to examine them will be surprised and may well think that he has found the desired entry to the other sea, or a ready means by which to penetrate for many leagues into the interior of the mainland, but all his hopes will be dissipated when, without having noticed the least indication that the channel was about to end, he finds it closed by a barrier of mountains which form a semicircle round it, and which invariably leave only a narrow beach up which it is impossible to advance for more than a few paces.

It would certainly be impossible to find a more delightful view than that which is here presented by the diversity of trees and shrubs, by the loveliness of the flowers and the beauty of the fruit, by the variety of animals and birds. When to this is added the pleasure of listening to the song of the birds, the observer is afforded many occasions for admiring the works of nature and for delighting his senses as he contemplates the majestic outlines of the mountains, covered with pines and capped with snow, when he sees the most glorious cascades falling from them and reaching the ground below with an awe-inspiring rapidity, breaking the silence of these lonely districts, and by their united waters forming powerful rivers which serve to give life to the plants on their banks, and in which a large number of salmon are bred. When any men are met, although they are of a different appearance and colour, it is clear that they are of the same species from the similarity of their ideas, and the observer will see that, denied those advantages which are believed to be indispensable for life, these men are yet very intelligent, strong and cheerful, and that, without the aid which is supplied by the study and perfection of the arts, they still know how to provide themselves with the necessary sustenance, to supply their wants and to defend themselves against their enemies.

The northern arm of the channel which we called Floridablanca and which the natives call Sasamat, ends in a river little worthy of notice, which flows down the slopes and through the gorge of a great mountain. Its source appears to be the melting snows, the water from which falls into it. Our officers who explored this channel wished to go up the river, despite the fact that it was very narrow, and navigating in half a fathom of water they were in danger of finding their boats caught in the trees which were on the banks. These trees formed an attractive wood in which there were some clearings, and near them a number of Indians who were amazed to see vessels so novel in appearance to them, and men even more strange, who appeared in that remote place, the entrance to which was assuredly hidden from all who were not filled with a vehement desire to make discoveries and led on by an unwearied curiosity. But neither the great distance from an inhabited land, nor the complete absence of all trade and means of communication among these people, who lived contented with the products of that barren land, nor the darkness and obscurity of the place in which they lived sufficed to preserve for them their lonely peace. The women fled at once and hid themselves among the rocks, while some of the men embarked in a canoe, accompanied by one boy to whom all showed great deference. They approached our boats, observing those who were in them, but in a little while returned to land, and went away into the wood.

The schooners, which should have set sail to join the English vessels, waited only for the return of the boats, and when this had occurred they set out at eight o'clock on the morning of the twenty-fifth, with a light easterly wind, and made all possible speed to effect the junction.

At two, a vessel was sighted on the horizon to south-east, and an hour later another smaller ship was sighted. We had no doubt that these were the English vessels, as in fact they were, and we approached them with the more speed as they were also making towards us. The corvette, which came ahead of the brigantine by a considerable distance, changed her course when she was near the *Sutil*. Galiano and Valdés, wishing to show respect to the commander, Vancouver, went on board, and there spent a large part of the afternoon.

The corvette *Discovery* seemed to be a vessel well fitted for the purpose of her voyage; the brigantine *Chatham* was very unsightly. Both ships were sheathed in copper and their hulls were much polished. The schooners made every effort to keep with them, but owing to their slower speed were always somewhat behind them.

The wind fell in the evening and at nightfall changed to the west; we hauled to the wind in the direction of the coast towards the north until we reached that part and then we tacked, but when the wind veered soon afterwards to south-west we tacked to port. The wind freshened and there were some showers, and although it looked as if dirty weather were coming up from the south-east with rain clouds, no ill consequences followed. The wind afterwards changed to south and then followed a west quarter south-west course, making two miles by twelve o'clock.

During the rest of the night the wind was light from the south, and at daybreak it was almost calm. During the morning, however, it turned to east and east-south-east and became stronger as the day went on. We passed the entry of Mazaredo without examining it, as it had already been visited by the English. This, and the entrance of Carmelo, were, as has been said, two arms of the sea of great depth, but the fact that they were known to be closed destroyed their attraction and made their examination of no importance, while our means were also limited and for this reason were we bound not to employ them on explorations of small value. In the entries of Porlier we had found that there was little possibility of moving the schooners by rowing, and we were assured that our ships possessed no merit either as vessels of radius or as vessels of mobility.

All the morning we had navigated behind the English ships, making good progress with fair weather and a fresh wind. At midday it became overcast, but in the afternoon the sky cleared.

Having passed the channel which the island of Texada forms with the coast, we found ourselves in an archipelago, in which night overtook us; the wind had almost fallen away and we were left in a group of small islands, seeking an anchorage, and taking soundings continually. Finally, the English corvette found an anchorage, and passing the news to the brigantine, the latter informed us. We made our way to it, the line constantly in hand, and let go the anchor at twenty-six fathoms, with a rocky bottom, to the south of an island which was afterwards called Quema because a fire had been made on it. The *Mexicana* was nearer the land and found thirty-six fathoms at hardly a cable's distance from the *Sutil*, and anchored in twenty-eight. This anchorage was of service merely in so far as it saved us from being left during the night at the mercy of the currents in a place of which nothing was known, but it was finally necessary to find a way to the mainland, as we were at present in an archipelago of islands, lofty and precipitous, between which there appeared to be channels of great depths.

CHAPTER IX

Valdés goes in the launch and explores Tabla and Arco channels and the entrances near.—The English are not prepared to leave unexplored the channels which we had already visited, on the ground that to do so would not be in accordance with their instructions.—Galiano explores the continent from Point Aarmiento to Tabla channel.—Vernaci and Salamanca continue the examination to beyond Angostura de los Comandantes.

THE dawn was fine, and methods were taken to combine our activities with those of the English. Captain Vancouver proposed to send out three expeditions, each consisting of two boats, in different directions, and Galiano suggested to him that we should have charge of one of these. Valdés therefore set out at nine in the morning in the launch of the *Mexicana* with provisions for eight days, and made his way along the channel which afterwards received the name of Tabla, his duty being to explore that part of it which lay towards the east.

The boat of the *Chatham* also set out with her captain, Mr. Broughton, who went to an entry which lay to the north-west. He returned at eleven with the information that there was a better anchorage in that channel than that at which we were lying. At half-past eleven, Mr. Vancouver, Galiano, Mr. Pujet, the second lieutenant of the corvette, and a midshipman, who always accompanied Vancouver, went to the south-west point of the island to observe the latitude and found a difference of 20″ on the same meridian.

At three in the afternoon, Mr. Vancouver came to the *Sutil*, bringing with him the artificial horizon, and Galiano and Vernaci embarked with him, taking the circular instrument and the lense on which it was mounted in order to make observations and test the glasses, landing for this purpose on a beach which there was on the nearest island. A southerly squall caused the corvette to drag her anchor and compelled Mr. Vancouver to go back to her to take command; he issued orders that she should proceed to the anchorage which had been found by Mr. Broughton, and this was done.

The *Mexicana* also tended to drag her anchor; the *Chatham*, whose sails were furled, fouled her cable, and the *Sutil*, which was under sail, heeled over at every gust of wind. We all hauled to the wind, which was southeast and veering to east, driving us towards the shore. We entered the channel, which is formed by very lofty mountains, and having proceeded about a league along it, we anchored in a safe place which was afterwards called La Separación.

At nightfall Valdés returned in the launch, having explored a considerable arm of the sea, which he called Tabla, because on the coast to the east he had seen on the shore a kind of wooden plank, on which were drawn various geographical figures, as was clear from the sketch which he made of it. This channel at first seemed to be of considerable importance and to extend for several leagues, but Valdés soon found that its end came when he least expected it, in just the same way as we had found in the case of the arm of the Floridablanca channel, to which this channel was similar both in the character of its shores and in its depth. He also visited the neighbouring channels, which are filled for the most part with small islands of little height, and he saw some abandoned settlements without having met a single native beyond them.

On his return from the examination of the arm of the sea called Tabla, Valdés met Mr. Pujet, second lieutenant of the *Discovery*, who was also on his way to explore the same channel, and although he told him that it was blocked, the English officer continued to go to explore it for himself.

In view of this, we explained to Captain Vancouver that the way in which exploration could be accelerated would be for us to repose complete confidence in one another and that so far as we were concerned, he could count on absolute frankness. Mr. Vancouver, however, replied that while he had always the most complete confidence in our work, he did not feel himself to be free from the responsibility if he did not see everything for himself, since it was expressly laid down in his instructions that he was to explore all the channels along the coast from 45° to Cook River.

From the twenty-eighth of June to the first of July we replenished our water and wood, and undertook astronomical observations for the rectification of the chronometers. The wind varied greatly in its direction and strength; at times, when it was south-east, it caused us to yaw until we were in forty fathoms' depth. The tide was very irregular, the wind having much effect both upon its strength and upon its duration. When it blew from the south-east the current flowed rapidly from this direction, and when the wind remained steady from that quarter the water rose and fell without changing its course. This phenomenon was also noticed in the channels of the Strait of Magellan, where there has been noticed a difference of five fathoms in two hours, without any change in the direction of the tide.

On the second of July, the weather was lovely, and in the afternoon

Galiano went in the launch of the *Mexicana* to continue his investigations. He returned on the night of the fifth, after having charted carefully the whole coast lying between Point Sarmiento and the channel of Tabla, keeping very close to the shore of the continent. He found closed an arm of the sea which communicated with two bays which we named the bays of Malaspina and Bustamente. He also examined all the small creeks and inlets which lay within the area mentioned.

On the sixth, Vernaci and Salamanca went with the launch and the long-boat to continue their explorations towards the west. On the evening of the eighth, with a fresh south-east wind, they entered an inlet which they called Quintano, and as a point of the coast prevented them from charting the whole shore of the large creek in which it ended, they were caught on the lee shore and tossed about in the surf. As they were tacking, several waves washed over the launch and she was on the point of capsizing, but the canvas covering which had been placed at the bow to protect from the rain prevented her from being swamped. In this emergency they adopted the immediate remedy of setting her stern to the sea, pointing her bow towards the coast, where there were smaller waves. Eventually they were glad to shelter in a very small creek, where they passed the night; but it was not a peaceful time, since the force of the wind and sea was extraordinary, and the waves broke on the coast with a terrific roar.

The sky was overcast on the morning of the tenth, and they continued their labours with a smooth sea and a light wind, making their way to the channel which was noted in the chart as Angostura de los Comandantes, because it had been examined by Galiano and Valdés before they went to the place in the schooners. They saw a large settlement situated in the pleasant plain on the west point of the mouth of the channel of Quintano, and proceeded to coast along to the mouth of Angostura, where they noted that the sea ran out with extraordinary swiftness, and they made directly towards the south point of the entrance, mooring the vessels with their bows towards the land. In the neighbourhood there were a large number of canoes with two or three Indians in each, engaged in sardine fishing. The instrument which they used in this task was a rounded piece of wood some three yards long, one-third of which was studded with hooks. In this way, dropping this kind of wide-toothed comb into the sea, and making various draws with it, they caught the sardines on its hooks and gathered them into the canoes. Many of the natives approached our officers without showing the least nervousness. These men were of medium height, well built, strong, of darkish colour, and in their appearance, language, clothing and arms not different from those within the strait.

The number of natives who were in this area exceeded a hundred and forty persons, and they appeared to be the best situated of those living on the strait, since they were established on the slope of a small hill with plains immediately near them, and had a land which was fertile and lovely. The fields and woods, full of trees, shrubs and smaller plants, supplied them with a great quantity of fruit of different kinds, which enabled them to vary their diet and to correct the acidity resulting from eating fish and shell-fish. There were also a number of wild animals and birds, and the coasts near afforded them various species of valuable fish.

As soon as Vernaci and Salamanca learned that the strength of the current had lessened, they passed Angostura and entered the creek near, the savages acting as guides. They discovered an entrance which led to various channels, but the Indians declaring that one of these led to the sea, they resolved to postpone its exploration and to return to the point which they had entered. They accomplished this by nightfall, availing themselves for their return of the time during which the strength of the currents was less. Although the channel which had been explored was so exposed on account of the great eddies produced by the current, they resolved to go through it with the schooners, since the small size of our boats did not allow them to proceed to any great distance from the ships.

On the twelfth, an expedition consisting of two English boats returned with news that an outlet to the sea had been found by it at 51° north. On account of this, the English commander told us that it was his intention to leave the channel in which we were anchored in order to follow another which was to the south-west and which, judging from its direction, should communicate with that which had been examined. He added that this channel was suitable for ships, and that the one which we proposed to follow was very dangerous, since it was full of shoals and had many currents and eddies. We explained to him that the small size of our vessels made it practicable for them to navigate this passage, and accordingly it was settled that we should separate.

CHAPTER X

Parting from the English vessels.—Vain attempts of the schooners to make progress.—Anchorage of Marias.—Anchorages of Ceballos, Robredo, Murphy and Concha.—Good character of the Indians of Angostura de los Comandantes.—Great force of the current there.—The schooners pass through and anchor in Refuge Creek.

At daybreak on the thirteenth there was a fairly strong westerly wind. The English vessels left and Mr. Vancouver continued his voyage, returning by the same channel in a south-easterly direction. We parted with many expressions of friendship and mutual confidence, and the commanders of the two expeditions mutually presented each other with copies of the explorations which had been achieved up to that point.

As the wind was unfavourable, we delayed our departure until the tide began to come in, which was at eight in the morning, and then prepared to sail, but seeing that all our efforts to make progress were vain, we returned to the anchorage which we had left.

On the fourteenth, after taking the sun, we set sail to avail ourselves of the favourable current, although the wind blew strongly from the north-west. We headed to the wind all the morning, making from shore to shore, being now near one, now the other, in order to escape the opposing eddies and to make use of such as were favourable. Even so, however, we were able to make only about half a mile, and a great part of this we lost on our two last tacks against the contrary tide, and we anchored on the north-east coast in twenty-five fathoms, with a sandy, shelly bottom.

Despite the fact that the weather on the fifteenth was similar to that of the previous days and promised no better results, whatever efforts we might make against it, we none the less set sail at eight in the morning, and kept to the wind without any gain, until we found that we were losing ground, when we anchored at half-past two in the afternoon on the south-west coast very near the point whence we had started.

The same unfavourable conditions prevailed on the sixteenth, except that the in-coming tide made it possible to change our course, the wind being steady in the north-west. This discovery confirmed us in the idea which we have already mentioned that there is no regularity in the tide in these channels. That which is in the same direction as the wind is strong, but that which is opposed to it, being held back by the wind, can hardly be observed. In the night we noticed that the tide from the southeast had force enough to move the ship, although the wind was not less strong. We hoped that the coming day would offer us greater promise than had the days previous, but as the tide was against us until ten in the morning we waited and at that hour set sail, continuing under canvas until two in the afternoon, when the wind which assisted us having fallen, we preferred to row very close to the shore in order to free ourselves from the force of the current. In this way we reached the anchorage of the three Maria Islands, after great exertions on the part of the crew. In the night the wind freshened somewhat, and there was no noticeable current, but in the morning we found it very strongly against us. The latitude was taken by two observations of the sun, on land and on board, the variation of the compass from the theodolite was marked, and notes were made for the continuation of our geometric survey.

In the evening we rowed the vessels as on the previous day, tending towards the coast on the right hand, where there were sure to be anchorages better protected. The tide gave us little help, and now and then opposing eddies had considerable power, so that it was with great exertion that we could row against them. We anchored at nightfall between the coast and the island which we called Ceballos, pointing our bow to land, and the anchors being dropped in twenty-six fathoms with a shelly bottom. From a settlement which was on the island, three canoes came out with as many natives in each one, and made their way to the *Sutil*, where they were treated with much friendliness. They replied by giving us to understand that it was not well that we should continue to follow this channel, as there were along it evil men who would murder us, and they urged us to come to their settlements, where they would supply us with the best entertainment. In the case of the *Mexicana* they made equal efforts to induce us to change our course, showing so consistently friendly and compassionate a spirit and such disinterested affection that we were unable to thank them sufficiently.

After having made the necessary observations on the morning of the seventeenth, at two in the afternoon, with the change to a favourable tide we continued rowing in the same conditions as on the previous days. At first the current carried us along rapidly, but as soon as we had come near the shore on the left hand, we met with variable cross currents, which were generally opposed to us, so that in the end we were compelled to anchor in a creek to which we gave the name Robredo, in thirty-five fathoms, having also a cable on land as on the previous occasions. We passed the night in peace, and in the morning at nine with a favourable tide we set out in search of Angostura de los Comandantes, close to which we fancied that we must be. The launch was sent to examine the state of the tide, but seeing that it was flowing against us, we anchored in sixteen fathoms in the anchorage of Murphy, in order to examine closely this dangerous situation and to equip ourselves with all information. For this purpose, the two commanders embarked in the launch, and steered towards the centre of the current, which they ceased to feel as soon as they had doubled the point of the creek in which the schooners were anchored. The extreme rapidity which the waters attained was a phenomenon worthy of the greatest attention. The current of Angostura de la Esperanza in the Strait of Magellan is seven and a half miles an hour near the shore, and its velocity is much greater in mid-channel. Nevertheless, the difference between the two currents, which can be noticed at once, is so great that it is no exaggeration to say that the current in Angostura de los Comandantes has a velocity of twelve miles. The sight is most strange and picturesque: the waters flow as if they were falling from a cascade; a great number of fish are constantly rising in them, and flocks of gulls perch on the surface at the entrance of the channel, allowing its rapid flow to carry them along, and when they have reached its end, they fly back to their original position and repeat the experience. This not only amused us, but it also supplied us with a means by which to gauge accurately the force of the current.

The Indians received the commanders with the greatest friendliness, and gave them to understand that they should not run the risk of attempting to navigate the channel in the launch, since they would inevitably be swamped in the whirlpools in it, as had happened to them with their canoes when they had the misfortune to be caught by the current. Galiano and Valdés replied by thanking them for their warning and then directed their attention to the discovery of means by which the schooners might be freed from so difficult a situation.

They noticed that it was clear that when the current was contrary in Angostura it was favourable on the coast on which the schooners were lying and as far as the point on the left hand, because the current, owing to the force with which it flowed on entering the channel, took the direction of the channel of Quintano, and the waters on the coast, on the left hand, flowed to fill the resultant space in order to maintain an exact level.

They found that at a cable from the said point there was an anchorage which they called Concha, in fifteen fathoms with a shelly bottom formed of the deposits which the water left as it lost its velocity on coming out of the channel, and from this fact they realised at once that it would be well that the schooners should anchor in that neighbourhood as being the best point at which to await the change of the current, in order to attempt the passage at the turn of the favourable tide, before the waters attained their extreme rapidity, when it would be dangerous to attempt it. They returned to the schooners and set to work immediately to put this plan into operation.

The Indians, indicating the course of the sun, signed to us that the favourable moment for which we longed would come when the sun was near the peak of a high mountain on the continent. The time passed quickly with the entertainment afforded by watching the rush of waters, the many trees which were washed down by its violence, the continual passage of the birds, and the play of the fish which churned the water where we were anchored.

The natives removed to some distance from the schooners without in any way lessening their friendly attentions; on the contrary they gave unequivocal proofs of their interest in our welfare, since in addition to presenting us with the first fresh salmon which we had seen in the strait and a great number of freshly caught sardines, they let few moments pass without making energetic signs to us of the dangers which we were about to encounter and the manner and time for overcoming them. They explained to us the method which they followed in making this navigation, and the continual mishaps which they none the less encountered, ending by making signs that the size and power of resistance of our vessels could not promise us any better fate, but rather one more unfortunate than that with which they met in their canoes. We responded to this humane and kindly conduct by calling them good Indians, and we were zealous in presenting them with whatever we thought might be for their pleasure or use.

At three o'clock the current began to lose force, and we observed that four was the moment for putting our hands to the work. We availed ourselves of the opportunity with all due energy, being accompanied for some while by our worthy friends, who also did not fail to warn us of the opportune moment or omit to escort us to mid-channel. From there, however, they returned hurriedly to their settlements, since the current began to gain strength. They still left a canoe with a man and a woman in it to afford us some guidance, without our having forced them to do so by any insistence on our part.

As soon as we were in the passage of Angostura we appreciated the necessity of not omitting to take every precaution against some unfortunate accident, in a place of which we had no sufficient knowledge to be aware of its dangers, and to take all means for avoiding such mischances. We accordingly resolved to anchor in the creek to the right in order from there to examine a sufficiently difficult part which was presented to our view and which we called the channel of Carvajal in gratitude to our friend Don Ciriaco Gonzalez Carvajal, oidor of the audiencia of Mexico, to whom our commission owed the performance of some special services. In order to carry out our intention we were bound to escape being drawn to the left side, where the officers Vernaci and Salamanca had observed some whirlpools so violent that the water was cast up more than a yard. We endeavoured constantly to follow the right shore, with the aid of oars, but the current carried us forward, bringing us sometimes to this shore and at others driving us to mid-channel, without our being able with all our efforts to avoid these variations of course. The *Mexicana* finally made the desired anchorage, but the *Sutil* was caught by a rush of the current and was not able to achieve the same result, and sailing more than three cables nearer the shore was almost caught on the rocks which jutted out from it. She entered the channel of Carvajal, allowing herself to be carried by the violence of the waters, since the resistance which had been made had proved to be useless, and adopted the course of continuing on her course under light sail to await the *Mexicana*. She soon afterwards set sail and followed the *Sutil*, experiencing the same fate, appearing as if she were out of control.

The schooners made the passage of Angostura with extraordinary speed, taking the wind with the studding sail, as it was blowing strongly in the opposite direction from that of the channel. The *Sutil* having steered to a point near an island, changed to the opposite course, and being caught by the force of a strong eddy, turned round three times with such violence that it made those who were in her giddy. Her crew freed her from this danger, rowing with all their might, and both schooners steered towards the right-hand coast with the intention of finding there a place to anchor before night came on, that being already very near, since then the current would gain its greatest force and increase the difficulties and dangers of this voyage.

The continual cross currents and eddies, sometimes in favour and sometimes against the schooners, now driving them back and now driving them forward, making it always impossible to control them and leaving them at the mercy of the waters, alternately raised and mocked our hopes of making a creek which was very near. The *Sutil* attempted to reach with the boat a point which was to the east, but at that moment was caught by another violent whirlpool and again carried along, breaking the end of the cable which was just being made fast. Finally at half-past nine at night we succeeded in finding an anchorage at Refuge Creek, both vessels lying under the shelter of a point which protected them from the wind, which had fallen, the anchor being in twenty fathoms with a shoally bottom and moored to the land.

Much later the wind increased in strength, so that we heard it whistling through the plants above us and through the trees on the mountain. At the same time the violent flow of the waters in the channel caused a horrible roaring and a notable echo, this producing an awe-inspiring situation, so that we had so far met with nothing so terrible.

CHAPTER XI

Difficulty caused by contrary currents near Refuge Creek.—Examination of Refuge Creek and Aliponzoni Creek.—The *Mexicana* leaves and makes the latter anchorage.—The *Sutil* finds the eddies, which are always to be met at Refuge Creek, very strong.—She overcomes them successfully, and both ships moor at Tenet anchorage.—Salamanca goes through Engaño Channel and follows the coast of the continent, until he has completed the exploration of both shores of the sound bearing his name.—The schooners leave and reach the anchorage of Viana.

THE ships proceeded to investigate the continuation of the channel and found an anchorage at Aliponzoni Creek suitable as a starting-point for further advance, but it was found that the appropriate hour for removing to it was passed for that day.

As darkness began to come on, the wind gathered force and blew strongly all night. The Indians did not appear, nor were there any signs that those shores were inhabited; this was the reason of the terror inspired by the misfortunes which had been experienced in that quarter.

For the whole of the twenty-second, the wind maintained the same force and was equally unfavourable, affording us no opportunity for availing ourselves of the turn of the tide in the morning in order to double the point to our north-west and reach the anchorage mentioned. At a suitable moment, the long-boat had been sent to examine the nature of the current and had not actually found it contrary. We waited for one of those occasional falls in the wind which occurred in order to start, but no such fall took place until half-past seven in the morning, and at that time we found that the tide was running towards the north-west with such speed that it was immediately clear that it would be impossible to overcome its force. The waters from Angostura de la Comandantes follow the Carvajal Channel, and while they continue in the same direction on the left-hand shore, they do not do so on the right-hand, but on reaching the extreme west point of the island, where the schooner *Sutil* was so violently tossed about, they divide, and after developing some whirlpools some go towards Aliponzoni Creek and others, producing a strong eddy, go towards the point of this name, and then back to the anchorage of Refuge Creek.

The periodic tide which we had observed in Carvajal Channel began to run out at half-past six in the evening. The gusts of wind had not entirely ceased, but they were not so violent as they had been on the previous day, and as we eagerly desired to continue our voyage, even at the cost of running some probable risks, we set out at seven in the evening. The *Mexicana*, which was farther out than the *Sutil*, had first to undertake the task, and she achieved it, proceeding for a considerable distance with her oars. The *Sutil* followed her at some three cables' distance, and this short distance was sufficient to enable the *Mexicana*, although with difficulty, to make Eddy Point, without the *Sutil* meeting with equal good fortune. The backwash increased when she was already near the point and carried her rapidly on to the shoal which is a cable east of the point, and then bore her towards the coast. In order to clear from it, it was necessary to use her oars as punt poles, and despite the energetic manner in which this resource was employed, the eddies carried her to Refuge Creek. The effort was then repeated: caught by the currents and whirlpools, she was carried to Eddy Point with such speed that it seemed to be vain to make any attempt to avoid running on the coast, but the waters themselves bore her to Refuge Creek. The effort was repeated a third and a fourth time in vain, and at last, despairing of accomplishing that which had clearly been so often prevented by the currents, she anchored. The *Mexicana* had moored in Aliponzoni Creek.

On the twenty-third, at six in the morning, the *Sutil* renewed her effort to leave, and with the experience of the previous evening and the knowledge gained concerning the character of this place, she rowed along in calm water near the coast, made Eddy Point, passed out of Aliponzoni Creek and on sighting the *Mexicana* at once joined her. With a fresh north wind in our favour, we then navigated along the left-hand shore.

When we had emerged from this perilous situation, we found more natives, who came alongside the *Sutil* in two canoes, telling us the course which we should follow. They displayed as much confidence as if they were with their greatest friends, and as we had shown them the chart of our explorations, they indicated to us on it by means of a pencil the course of the channels which appeared to the west and those which had an outlet to the sea. As they did not understand the manœuvre of tacking, in the course of which we were at times proceeding in the direction opposite to that which was to be followed, they advised us not to steer towards Estero Creek, as it was closed, indicating how the sides formed a bow. But when they found that we paid no attention to their advice, they went off to the shore. We tacked as far as Estero Creek, found that it was entirely closed, and stood towards the narrow channel of Engaño, which leads north-west, arriving at its entrance. When, however, we prepared to enter it, a canoe full of our Indian friends came up and told us that it had no outlet. The favouring tide was now ceasing and we accordingly steered towards the west coast, in order to seek an anchorage in Novales Channel, and we anchored in the bay of that name at a cable from land.

The information concerning these waters supplied to us by the Indians did not agree with that which we had received from the English, and it was thus essential that the smaller vessels should proceed to examine Engaño Channel. For this purpose, Salamanca set out in the launch at half-past two in the afternoon with a favourable tide which carried him northwards towards the coast.

On the twenty-fourth the weather became overcast, and on the twenty-fifth we had a south wind with rain and clouds. We spent this time in making such observations as the clouds permitted, and on the work necessary for the continuation of the charting of these coasts. The launch returned at night, and Salamanca informed us that he had surveyed the Engaño Channel, one arm of it which ran northwards and ended in a river, and the deep bay which led to the west. With a south wind, he traversed the whole of the channel named after him; he saw a native settlement and two rivers of considerable importance, the mouths of which suggested that they were sheltered. He certainly learned that the points of land jutting out at intervals produced a false impression: at a distance of half a mile they commonly hid the entrances of large channels, and as a result of this discovery he was led to proceed for over fourteen leagues in a northerly direction, and ventured to cross to the opposite shore in order to be better able to investigate the mouths of the rivers. Despite the fact that the wind was contrary and blowing strongly, he attempted to enter the channel to the east, but found that the entrance to it was blocked by a fishing pool, excellently made with stakes and planks. Both entrances were wide but very shallow, and the current was so swift that it would have been rash to face it with so small a vessel, which would have been at the mercy of the waters. The natives of the settlement there had observed our launch, and when they saw that it did not come nearer they came out in two canoes, with eight or ten men in each, shouting and showing an otter skin. Our men could not wait for them as the launch was in a critical position, and orders were given to make sail for the coast to the east in order to avoid the waves which dashed upon the shore and which the boat could not have ridden. This action would seem to have excited the suspicion of the Indians and have caused them to think that our men were hostile, for they returned to their settlement, put on their war dress, re-embarked and, joining a canoe in which was a tais, followed the launch, in which Salamanca at once prepared to make use of such feeble means of defence as were at the disposal of our men. The braves landed and followed the launch on shore, displaying alternately otter skins and arrows, until they could follow no farther, when they returned to their settlement. As it was growing dark, our men found a small creek, to which they made their way in order to pass the night, a time which was very unpleasant as it rained heavily. On the twenty-fifth, the sky cleared and Salamanca returned by the way he had come, continuing his geodetical labours.

At eight on the morning of the twenty-sixth and at the favourable turn of the tide we set sail, and aided sometimes by our oars and at others by the south wind we made the mouth of Engaño Channel. We passed through it, rowing between the island and the south coast, choosing to proceed by this narrow channel rather than by the larger open channel to the north. The current, which had considerable force, was in our favour and we reached the point where the channel turns west-south-west, then we at once found an east-south-east wind which carried us along rapidly while we were opposite Olavinde Channel. There the wind dropped and we let ourselves float with the current, and with the help of our oars proceeded towards the entrance of Cordero Channel. Such, however, was the force of the eddies and whirlpools that they carried the *Mexicana* on to the north-east point of the channel with a force that seemed to be likely to break her up on it. The current bore the water with violence against the shore; the shore cast them back, and the two schooners proceeded to anchor at two in the afternoon in Viana Creek in twenty-four fathoms with a shelly bottom at a cable and a half from land.

It had rained unceasingly all day: during the night it was again squally, and there was every indication that the winds were changing to south-east, so that they would be favourable for our course.

CHAPTER XII

The schooners leave and pass through the Channel of New Whirlpools.—The launch is employed as a guide: they follow it and reach the anchorage of Novales.—Valdés examined the Canonigo Bay and Flores Bay.—The schooners proceed and pass on to the anchorage of Banza.—Some knowledge of the language of Nootka is found among the natives.—The ships proceed to continue their voyage and moor in the anchorage which is called Insult on account of that which the natives did to our men.—Vernaci is despatched in the launch to make various surveys, and he carries them out successfully.

WE started at seven in the morning of the twenty-seventh, and with some wind from the east proceeded to the north of the channel of New Whirlpools. The launch was manned, and with it as our pilot we pursued our course through the channel, but in passing through the narrow part of it, which is midway, we met with whirlpools which obliged us to leave ourselves at their mercy. Having passed them successfully, and having found several inlets to the north, we reached a good anchorage at eleven o'clock and called it Novales. Its latitude was taken on land; the sun was taken, and the launch went with Valdés to examine the inlets which were in sight.

He returned on the twenty-eighth, having surveyed Canonigo Bay and Flores Bay, and having found that the channel ran to the west, we at once started and profited from the tide until its turn obliged us to anchor in twenty-four fathoms with a muddy bottom in the anchorage of Banza. During most of the day it was wind still, and the tendency of the clouds on the horizon to disperse gave promise of a westerly breeze.

Several natives appeared in three canoes in the evening, and some of them understood the language of Nootka, especially one who immediately acted as interpreter in our dealings with them. They knew Macuina and other chiefs of that district, and the very way in which they regarded the articles of barter and the manner in which they conducted the exchanges made showed that they had dealings with the people of that country.

On the morning of the twenty-ninth, we continued our course with a fresh west wind and a favourable tide, making to the west from the hope that we should soon reach an outlet to the sea. Already we noticed a change in the character of the land: it was less rugged and lower; to the north-west there was a wide open sky, and extensive beaches were to be seen, with good anchorages by them. In the afternoon the wind freshened and the sea rose, but the breeze soon dropped and we were almost becalmed. The natives did not fail to visit us, and thereby our stock of fresh and dried salmon was increased: they took in exchange iron, shells and some trifles.

By tacking we made the anchorage of Cardenas, and as an inlet appeared to the north, we moored in twelve fathoms with a fine gravelly bottom, in order to go in the launch to examine it.

When this had been done on the morning of the thirtieth, we set sail with a strong east wind, running along the north coast at such a distance from it that no inlet large enough to allow the passage of a canoe could be hidden from us. At four in the afternoon a channel was seen and the schooners anchored very near its mouth, at an anchorage which was afterwards named Insult, owing to that which the Indians who inhabit its shore did to us.

As we came to anchor, several canoes with natives in them ran alongside the schooners. The majority of these Indians understood the language of Nootka and they showed that they had had many dealings with Europeans, from whom they had acquired various articles. A tais wore a hat very like that which we had in the previous year seen the chief at Mulgrave Harbour, at 60°, wearing; he prized it greatly because he had secured it in a battle from his enemies. We bought it, and it was the only thing that we could obtain, because the natives, entirely uncertain rather than cautious in their dealings, refused whatever we offered to them, except such things the use of which they knew for themselves, and which seemed to be more to their taste.

At daybreak on the thirty-first, Vernaci went in the launch to examine the inlet which ran towards the north, in order to determine its exact extent: according to our position, it might possibly lead to the sea. Most of the men were afterwards ordered ashore to collect wood, in order to make new oars, and for other special purposes.

At midday we heard shouts and saw several canoes collected near the place where our men were working. Salamanca at once entered the boat with armed men and went to their help with the intention of doing no injury to the hostile natives except in an extreme case. We discharged a small cannon and its noise, coupled with the sight of the muskets in the boat, produced a good result, for the natives immediately entered their canoes and crossed the channel, keeping at a good distance from the schooners.

As our people afterwards informed us, the natives had surprised them and had attempted to take by force a musket which one of the woodcutters had, and they only abandoned their attempt when they saw the rapidity with which effective help was coming to those whom they had attacked and on account of their just fear of the slaughter which our firearms would cause among them.

The rain, which was incessant on the afternoon and the night following, filled us with concern about the launch, since it was bound to be greatly inconvenienced. We thought that some further trouble with the natives might have occurred to those in her. Most of the Indians who came in sight were armed, not only with arrows and machettes, but also with knives, a foot to half a yard long, with two shafts and a sharp point, and all this increased our concern for Vernaci and the people who had gone under his command.

On 1 August, in the morning, two Indians came in a canoe and said that they were Nuchimases and that they belonged to a different settlement from that to which those who had attacked us the day before belonged. They carried a musket which was in fairly good condition, a lance with an iron head three-quarters of a yard long, and some large knives with grooves in the middle of the blade and similar in every way to those used by the Indians living at 59° north and 60° north. They willingly allowed us to examine them and told us that they made them themselves. It was impossible to buy anything from them, as they were not willing to accept anything except powder in exchange. They landed with our men while we watched them, and they went away, not returning all day.

It was fine on the morning of the second, and at midday we made an observation of the latitude with the artificial horizon. Not a single canoe was seen, and this increased our anxiety concerning the launch, on which the natives would have easily been able to work their will, overcoming all those who were in her.

At three in the afternoon, a very high wind suddenly rose and ended in a heavy downpour of rain, which lasted all the rest of the afternoon and for a great part of the night.

The weather on the third was exactly the same, except that the tempest in the afternoon was accompanied by thunder and lightning. On this day we observed a phenomenon which we were very far from expecting to see. The mercury used for preparing artificial horizons had become mixed with moisture, and it was necessary to find some way in which to get rid of this. Various methods which were tried proved to be useless, and it was decided to boil it in a casserole in order to get rid of the moisture by these means, which were known to be effective. The desired result was certainly produced, but a man of fifty years of age, who was entrusted with the duty of stirring the metal while it was on the fire, became attacked with pains, on which fever followed and a copious and continual sweat as if he were really suffering from high fever. He was treated as if he were, and after some while happily recovered.

On the fourth there came alongside a canoe in which was Cauti, a young man of good presence, who told us that he was a tais of the Nuchimas and powerful in that district. He brought us news of the launch, which he related with vivacity and in a naturally agreeable manner, explaining everything very well in the Nootka language. We went on to talk with him of Macuina and some other chiefs of that district whom he knew. As we thought that it would be very advantageous to us to secure the friendship and confidence of this chief, we entertained him suitably on both vessels, with the result that he went away very pleased and offering to return accompanied by another tais, called Sisiaquis, lord of some lands lying on the northern shore.

The weather continued to be of the same character as it had been on the previous days, and at the same time on each day we had similar storms and tempests.

On the morning of the fifth, Cauti came in fulfilment of his promise, accompanied by Sisiaquis, and we received them with all the cordiality which our concern at the delay in the return of the launch suggested to us. Sisiaquis, after he had been with us for some while, told us that on that night he would sleep on shore near, and that he would return next day to receive the presents which we offered him.

We were now greatly troubled about the fate of those who had gone in the launch, since, as they had taken few provisions, we could feel sure that a large part of them must have been spoiled by the rains and sea water; we were accordingly assiduous in making presents to Sisiaquis and in gratifying him, as his help might, in the circumstances, be valuable to the men in the launch. This chief had with him some of his subjects, armed with muskets and with a good supply of ammunition and a horn full of powder. His confidence and ease of manner in nowise detracted from his nobility and power, of which he boasted, saying that Cauti was his inferior and that he was not recognised as his equal in those districts, which he assured us all belonged to him. He offered to entertain us if we went to his settlement, according to the custom of the taises, who trade only under cover of giving and receiving presents. He showed clearly that he had seen large vessels with three masts, although he did not reveal when or where this had been. After paying us a long visit, in which we found that our knowledge of the language of Nootka was very useful, Sisiaquis went away by the large channel which ran west-north-west, and one of the canoes of those who accompanied him crossed to the southern shore. From these and other indications we inferred that this was where these Indians lived, and that they were those who had attacked us, the more so because Sisiaquis, fearing our just resentment, was eager to hide the fact.

Although the rains on the fifth were less heavy than they had been on the previous day, the downpours continued to occur at the same times as before. On the sixth the wind was very variable, with continual showers during the afternoon and night. The thought of our launch continued to make us feel depressed, and we necessarily feared that it had met with some misfortune. We accordingly considered a means by which we might go in search of her, and none seemed to be more suitable than to leave the *Mexicana* at the anchorage in case the launch should return, and to let the *Sutil* proceed along the coast of the mainland, discharging cannon at intervals and inquiring of the Indians concerning the boat. We were about to put this idea into practice, when at half-past six on the morning of the seventh we saw the launch in the channel to the west-north-west; it had not been sighted until it was quite close, owing to the fact that the horizon was covered with clouds.

Evidence that a way out to sea was near had impelled Vernaci to survey the end of these channels, contending against the wind and tide, the thick cloud and constant rain. He examined the arms which bear his name and those of Retamal, Balda and Baldinar, and ended his exploration in the Pinelo Channel, which is on the west coast of the last-named, six days after he had set out from the schooners. He observed the latitude with the artificial horizon at the end of the first arm, and did not pursue the examination as far as the outlet to the sea, which he believed to be very near, on account of various facts, including the number of whales which were spouting in the Pinelo Channel; he felt that he was too far from the schooners and also very few provisions remained.

He had seen districts which were attractive, consisting of lands of little height covered with trees and meadows, as well as many beaches where there was good anchorage near by, although there were rugged and very lofty mountains on the shores of the channel to which his name was given. He found one waterfall, produced by the melting snow, admirable; the waters collected in a mountain gorge and then fell with much noise into the channel, causing enough motion in the air to enable Vernaci to set the sails of the launch and to proceed for some distance with the wind produced in this way.

He also saw many native settlements near the rivers in which these arms normally ended, and to which the salmon which are plentiful on the coast went to spawn. He noticed that the Indians preferred this situation to the inner part of the strait, partly on account of the abundance of fish, and partly because it gave them greater opportunities for trading with strangers, from which the Nuchimases derived advantages which they valued highly.

Vernaci had carried with him so few articles of barter that the supply was exhausted on the first two days of his voyage, and at this he was sorry, because the Indians troubled him by continually asking him to give them some of the clothes in which they saw our men dressed, or the arms which they carried in the launch, offering in exchange skins or other things which they valued less. They were surprised when the launch entered the channels along which they had their settlements and were eager to discover what the object of the strangers was which caused them to follow such curious routes, and to proceed in such small numbers and in so small a vessel. They had seen that it was not with the desire of trading, since they had not sought to buy anything, and becoming full of confusion and uneasiness, they made signs that our men should not go farther. When our men indicated that they were going to see the end of the channel, they gave them to understand, using the language of signs and making it most expressive, that the channel was completely blocked. Becoming assured that they could not induce us to abandon our intention, some of them went ahead, shouting in order to warn the settlements inland that their inhabitants might be on their guard and make every preparation for their safety and defence. At moments Vernaci found himself in a very difficult position, in which he was doubtful which of many possible courses was the most prudent to take. He saw a considerable number of canoes coming towards the launch: the natives in them were full of impertinent curiosity: they wished to have everything that they saw, and among them were some who were very dexterous in stealing everything which was not given to them willingly. It was necessary to keep them from boarding the launch, both in order to prevent theft and also because our men might have been surprised and overcome if they had allowed their boat to be entered by men who were warlike, well supplied with bows, arrows and spears, and proud of their dominion over the channels which they navigate and of the lands lying on those channels which they own. It was not always enough merely to steer away from them; it was also necessary to show severity and to be ready to use our weapons in event of any attack being made, although this would have been equivalent to a declaration of war and would have had fatal consequences for the progress of our voyage. He was able to satisfy them all by his attitude towards them, although he could neither win them by presents nor meet their wishes, and he was able to examine all the shore of the mainland at close quarters. He induced them to see reason with the more energy in order to convince them that it was not in their power to seize the launch with impunity, as those who live at the entrance of those channels had attempted to do in the case of the packet-boat *San Carlos*, and as had been done in the case of the boat sent out in 1788 by Captain Meares with an officer and fifteen men.

Vernaci proposed not to return to the schooners by the way in which he had gone from them, as he believed that he had found another and shorter route and through an archipelago. According to the plan which he had formed, by following this course, he was bound greatly to reduce the length of the voyage, if he could find a passage among the islands of which the archipelago was formed. When, however, he was in their midst, he found that they were so numerous and formed so many channels of such intricacy that it was difficult to examine them in a short space of time. An Indian misled him by promising to show him the way out; as soon as he had brought the launch into the midst of the maze, this native vanished. Seeing himself to be in such a difficult position, the distress of which was accentuated by the rain and by the complete exhaustion of the supplies of food, he resolved to turn back, since, despite the fact that his voyage was lengthened by the need for finding again the passages by which he had entered, he would thus come to a part which was known and so return by the way that he had come; and this, in actual fact, he succeeded in doing.

At the entrance to the Torres Channel, he had seen a gulf which ended to the west in an infinity of islands, and he conjectured that the channels formed by them would afford an outlet to the sea. Judging from the analogy of that which we had found in the case of all the channels in that part which had been surveyed, there was no reason for expecting that any valuable information would be acquired there, and that we should merely expose ourselves to risks by remaining in such high latitudes when the winter equinox was at hand in schooners of such defective construction. In these circumstances, it seemed to be more useful to employ the time that remained to us for our work on the exploration of Ezera Sound and in fixing the position of certain points on the south coast of Fuca Strait, especially the Santa Barbara channel. The year before, the corvettes *Descubierta* and *Atrevida* had visited some of the islands which form that channel, and from their observations gathered that they were incorrectly marked on our maps. These considerations led us to decide upon making a speedy return to the open sea, and rather to engage upon the tasks mentioned than upon the examination of new inlets and channels.

CHAPTER XIII

The schooners set out and proceed along the channel of Descubierta, in which they anchor.—They again set sail and go past the village of Sisiaquis.—Wealth of the Indians living there.—The English brigantine *Venus* is sighted.—Account of this vessel.—The schooners anchor near the settlements of Majoa and Quacos in the channel of Atrevida.—From there they proceed to survey the northern coast, but the mist hinders them and they anchor.—The cables break, and the ships proceed to Guemes Harbour.

AT six on the morning of the eighth we put out our oars, availing ourselves of the tide, and soon afterwards hoisted sail; the wind was variable in its force and direction. Although the sun was shining, a penetrating cold was felt at times.

We intended to anchor at nightfall under shelter of the islands on the north coast, where the boat found thirty-three fathoms with a gravelly bottom, but the depth was so unequal that the *Mexicana* had fifteen fathoms at her stern and thirty at her bow. The *Sutil* found bottom at forty fathoms, let go her anchor, which fell in fifty-five, and then proceeded with her oars, dragging her anchor along until it held fast. She was then moored to the land to make her secure.

At five on the morning of the ninth we set sail with an east wind, steady and fresh, with the help of which we made way against the tide, which was contrary to us throughout the morning. Sisiaquis came on board with two of his Indians and gave us to understand that Nootka lay to the south-east and that we could speedily reach that harbour by sea. He asked us to pass by his villages, where we could sleep; he said that he would make presents to us, and told us that his women would serve us as they had served other travellers, these travellers being, as he explained by signs, English merchants and traders, who paid the women for this kind attention by giving them a quantity of copper.

We presently saw a large settlement, built in the shape of an amphitheatre on a small hill, surrounded by an attractive meadow and close to a stream; it was laid out in streets, and from the sea presented an agreeable appearance because the houses were painted in different colours and adorned with good paintings. It was the best settlement which we had met with since that of Tetacus. In this numerous tribe, which, as we understood, is of the same race as the people of Nootka, there was evidence of the luxury which is the result of their active trading with Europeans and their constant relations with the Nuchimases. The Indians here repeated their request that our commanders should come to their houses, and when they were convinced that we were resolved not to lose time, they went off to their settlement and immediately returned, to the number of fifty, in several canoes in order to barter otter skins and some cloaks made of the bark of trees and grass, bordered in different colours, very evenly made and in good taste.

Since ten in the morning we had a brigantine in sight to the west; in the afternoon we came within hailing distance and learned that she was the *Venus*, Captain Henry Shepherd; she had come from Bengal and had called at the stations of Nootka and Fuca, and had met the men of our ships. Captain Shepherd conveyed to us the sad news that at Fuca the Indians had murdered the pilot of the frigate *Princesa*, Don Antonio Cerantes.

The brigantine only carried twenty-two men, most of whom were blacks from Jolo, wretchedly clothed and very unskilful in managing her; certainly no vessel could have been easier or better fitted for working than this ship, which was beautifully built. At her stern, above the bulwarks, she had a network, some two yards high, to guard against any Indian surprise attack, and she was well fitted with light ordnance and four small cannon. As night was beginning to fall, the three vessels anchored near the famous settlements of Quacos and Majoa; many canoes came out to all three ships, and in one of the canoes came the tais of Majoa, who proclaimed himself to be so, presenting a skin to the commander of each of the ships. They brought a large quantity of very good skins, and we bought some, rather to meet the importunate desires of the natives than for any advantage which was to be gained from the purchase of a type of skin which could be secured far more cheaply in the presidencies of California. The rate of barter which we were able to arrange was a sheet of copper of fourteen pounds for two skins, one good and the other moderate. As for the English captain, despite the economy and even parsimony with which he managed his voyage, he complained of the small profits which this trade produced.

The more the natives thronged to the schooners, the more careful were we to take precautions to guard against disputes with them, but we were not long in realising the value of this care on our part and the need for maintaining it. An accident caused us to see that to which we were exposed from the violent temper and impatience of these savages. One of our men quarrelled with an Indian, who immediately asked another native, who was among those in the canoes, for a knife and came on board the schooner *Sutil* to attack the sailor, whom he found awaiting him with his sabre drawn. All the Indians became restless and began to call their chief, who was in the cabin. It cost a great deal of trouble to quiet them and to maintain the peace until they went away at nightfall. These Indians are good-looking, well-proportioned, with a fierce mien and an easy carriage; they did not bring a single woman with them.

At dawn on the tenth we set sail for the northern coast, in order to survey it and fix its situation. Having crossed the Atrevida channel we found that it ended in many islands to the west; their appearance suggested that the way to the open sea was near. The weather was cloudy and rainy, and although the wind was strong from the south-east and aided us to run to good points for preparing the chart, the poor visibility hampered us, the land being hidden in mists. At twelve o'clock we actually arrived within half a mile of the north coast and found many Indians. The south-east wind beat upon it and was now very strong, with cloud and rain, so that we tacked across to the south coast in order to find an anchorage under shelter of it. We steered for a beach, beginning by finding twenty-five fathoms and a fine sandy bottom ; we went on until we were a cable and a half from this shore, and anchored broadside on to the land, to which we were moored, in six fathoms with a sandy and gravelly bottom.

It rained heavily during the night, the wind became stronger and the surf was so heavy that the schooners shipped water over the bow into the holds. It dropped at dawn, but we underran the cables and were in a distressed state. We at once proceeded to find a better anchorage, the wind being slight from the south-east but the rain being continuous and the mist being still thick. We followed the coast after clearing the islets which lay to our north-west, and finding an opening at a short distance, we entered it and found bottom at twenty-two fathoms, sandy and muddy. We called this anchorage Guemes Harbour, in honour of the viceroy of New Spain, the special protector of the expedition of our schooners.

There is another creek to the south-west of this harbour, but it would serve only for small boats as the entrance to it is shallow. The best anchorage for larger vessels is to the south-east; the northern coast is dirty; there is a river on it with good water and there are many places suitable for getting water in large quantities. The west coast offers a good beach for landing, and inland there are many herbs useful against scurvy, among which we saw the chilli, of which the taste is not unpleasant.

CHAPTER XIV

Stay of the schooners in Guemes Harbour.—Exploration of the Salida channel.—The schooners leave and make the anchorage of Mier.—They afterwards proceed to that of Villaviciencio.—They put out to sea and anchor between Point Sutil and Cape Scott.—Owing to a storm they run to Valdés Harbour, from which place they navigate to the harbour of Nootka.

It rained continuously on the eleventh and the wind was steady from the second quarter. The same weather, varied by some easterly gales, prevailed on the twelfth, but the security of our station relieved us of all anxiety and allowed us to enjoy the delightful food, which consisted in an abundance of soles, salmon, ray and a number of small fish similar to the Maluinas ling which abound on these shores and which we caught easily.

We made a prolonged stay in this harbour, since the wind, which was steadily south-east with continual showers of rain, left us no alternative. It was our belief that the way to the open sea was very close to us, and we were not inclined to select so unsuitable a time for the exploration of the western entrance to the strait and that part of the coast which lay between it and Cape Frondoso. A more rational way of employing the time to advantage was by regulating carefully the marine clocks, seizing upon those bright intervals when the sun was visible. At their previous anchorage the schooners had fretted one of their principal mooring ropes, so that only one which was satisfactory remained and a hempen cable. It was thus impossible for us to run the risk of attempting to find an anchorage near the outlet to the open sea in weather which was either unfavourable or at best uncertain.

The slight intercourse which we had with the Indians living on Guemes Harbour was devoid of profit save in that it enabled us to buy some fresh salmon; we could not glean from them any information of value. Their fishing ground lay in the creek to the south-west, and near it were some huts which they at times left deserted; they came to the schooners to barter, and as soon as they had done so, they made off. Very few of them visited us; they displayed a lack of intelligence which we had not found among those who lived at the settlement of Majoa, despite the fact that the natives at Guemes came from there. The difference may be due to the fact that they had little intercourse with others, living, as they did, in a deserted place.

When we had completed the observations required for the regulation of our marine clocks, Galiano went in the launch on the twenty-fifth to examine the channel which ran to the west; it was his purpose to find a good anchorage near the outlet to the sea, so that we could remove to it and then avail ourselves of the first north-west wind to proceed to Nootka. He ran along the whole south coast of the Salida channel without finding any anchorage until he reached the harbour which he called Gorostiza. After passing this point, he calculated the latitude and longitude in relation to Point Sutil and at a place very near that point, making use of the artificial horizon, by means of which he fixed the western mouth of the channel. He returned to the schooners at midnight.

On the twenty-third we set sail for the harbour of Gorostiza, using our oars at first and then proceeding under sail with a light east wind, so that we were close hauled until midday, when we were suddenly becalmed, after which the wind rose from the west, with violent gusts, strong squalls and much mist. We were unable to make the anchorage, and were thus obliged to put into the harbour of Salida in order not to pass the night tacking to and fro in so narrow a channel. Soon after we had put into harbour, however, the wind fell, the mist cleared and the sky began to assume a different aspect. This change having occurred, we felt that we ought not to lose the advantage which we had gained, and so the boat was sent to find an anchorage on the coast, which it did in twenty-six fathoms with a gravelly bottom. We proceeded to it and moored in the anchorage which we afterwards named Mier.

During the calm of early morning we made progress by rowing, until at nine o'clock the wind sprang up from the west. We then proceeded to tack for the whole morning, making some advance, and then after midday we began to fall to leeward. Being resolved not to lose that which we had gained, we sent the boat towards the north coast, where there was a good mooring-place in sight. This was, in fact, found to be very roomy and safe, and we steered to it, dropping anchor in twenty-five fathoms with a sandy and gravelly bottom in a creek which we named Villaviciencio Creek.

At daybreak we set out in search of the mouth of the strait, and as the wind soon began to blow strongly from the east, we made good progress. We saw lying at anchor on the north coast a sloop which did not answer our flag by showing hers. The sun being covered with cloud, we could not take observations, but it was certain that the outlet was well placed for the schooners. In order to gain exact knowledge of the coast, the *Sutil* proceeded very close to that on the north and the *Mexicana* to that on the south. The *Sutil's* boat examined Consolation Creek and another very safe sheltering place near the north point of the outlet, with a muddy bottom at from six to twenty-four fathoms; we called this anchorage Valdes Harbour. The force of the wind varied greatly, as did its direction; the sky and the horizon were cloudy. We waited to see what the weather would be before setting out, but as the wind rose from east to north-east, we made for the open sea.

At nightfall the sky was overcast, and we followed the lay of the coast by the light of the moon, anchoring in thirty fathoms with a bottom of fine black sand in a very suitable place for the continuation of our labours on the following morning.

At daybreak, despite the unfavourable weather outlook, we weighed anchor and steered so as to keep half a mile from land in sixteen fathoms with a gravelly bottom; we then ran along the coast towards Cape Scott with a very strong south-east wind.

We ran before it, coming out to the sound which is formed by the cape and the islands of Lanz, and at the passage to which we proceeded the wind turned to the south. We tacked under the mainsail in order to come near the coast, but the wind became so strong that it became the wisest course to return to the mouth of the strait and make Valdés Harbour. We accomplished this at two in the afternoon, when the sky already gave unmistakable signs that a storm was approaching which our frail vessels would be unable to resist. The solitude, the sombre aspect of the coast and the forbidding appearance of the mountains, which at other times were a depressing sight for us, were now a source of delight and relief, when we thought of the security which their protection afforded to us.

We knew that in order to gain the entry from a position to the south or west-south-west of the harbour and at no great distance from its mouth, it was necessary to make out two landmarks, one red and the other white, and clearly visible. We entered the mouth of the strait, which is two-thirds of a mile wide, and having passed an island we found a satisfactory anchorage in a semicircular space which seemed to be a natural harbour. The hills surrounding it, covered with thick woods, protect ships from violent winds, and the abundance of fish, with which the sea is churned, secures a variety of food and serves to amuse such as are fond of fishing.

As the bad and contrary weather continued, we remained at anchor until the morning of the thirteenth, when we set sail and, tacking, made our way out. Nightfall found us near Cape Boise or Frondoso, where we were off a part of the coast which had been already explored and charted by the corvettes *Descubierta* and *Atrevida* of our navy in the previous year. Hoisting all sail we availed ourselves of the wind, which blew very strongly behind us, and as day broke came in sight of the harbour of Nootka, in which we anchored at midday.

CHAPTER XV

Reflections on the slight practical value of the explorations made.—Account of that which had occurred in the harbour of Nootka during our expedition, and of the ships which had anchored there.—The vessels under the command of the English captain, George Vancouver, arrive at Nootka, and this officer produces the commission which he held from his court to take over the harbour of Nootka and the Spanish establishment there in the name of Great Britain.

WE arrived at Nootka four months after we had set out from that harbour, all this time having been spent in explorations, which in the main served only to satisfy curiosity, without being of any profit to navigators. When it had once been settled, as it was as a result of this exploration, that there was no passage to the Atlantic through the Fuca Strait, the gloomy and sterile districts in the interior of this strait offered no attraction to the trader, since in them there were no products, either of sea or land, for the examination or acquisition of which it was worth while to risk the consequences of a lengthy navigation through narrow channels, full of shoals and shallows. We did not see otters or other animals whose skins might set an edge on greed; the character of the land did not offer expectations that places would be found suitable for the formation of settlements or in which the winter could, in case of need, be passed. Only a philosopher might, perhaps, find in these districts food for reflection, seeing there a land and peoples so near to the primitive state of the world, so far removed from European civilisation, which they did not appreciate and for which they had no desire.

The fact that our expedition was of no great strength and the necessity of prosecuting, at all costs, hydrographical investigations, deprived us of the satisfaction which we might have derived from visiting the settlements and houses of the natives and from having with them that close intercourse by means of which alone it would have been possible to acquire knowledge of their character, of their customs and of their government. But so far as we were able to gather from the slight intercourse which we had with them it would seem that they vary greatly in disposition, for whereas some showed themselves to be affable, generous and trustful, others displayed exactly the opposite characteristics. It is true that, so far as we were concerned, they gave us no cause for complaint, except on the one occasion when they attempted to do us an injury, despite the fact that many times they felt themselves to have the advantage in their encounters with our launch, and it is also true that on many occasions we received from them service born of friendly feeling.

The government of these natives who live along the strait of Fuca and the channels leading from it, the internal economy of their settlements, their manufactures and dress, are very similar to those of the inhabitants of Nootka, whom we shall describe later on. We were unable to satisfy our curiosity concerning the use to which they proposed to put the great quantities of copper which they were acquiring; they used little of it for purposes of personal adornment, while they received a great deal in exchange for skins from the ships which engage in this trade. In recent years, this commerce has become very lucrative for them, the value of the skins having risen in proportion to the increase of consumption and as a result of competition among the buyers. Macuina said that in the year 1788 he had sold skins at the rate of ten for a sheet of copper to Captain Meares, and to-day the rate of exchange is a sheet of half an arroba in weight for each skin of the best quality. In our brief intercourse with the Nuchimases we did not find that they would give us three skins of normal size and quality for two sheets of copper of an arroba in weight.

The gain made by the English sailor George Dixon from the trade in skins along this coast aroused the greed of traders, who saw the increasing advantages which would accrue from it and which he explained in his account of his voyage. Hence, although various circumstances had contributed greatly to reduce the gains which were at first derived from this trade, by 1792 there were already twenty-two vessels engaged upon it, eleven being English, eight American, two Portuguese and one French, and the American, Mr. Gray, captain of the *Columbia*, had secured for himself alone a thousand skins. There was hardly a single point on the coast between 37° north and 60° north which had not been visited by these ships, and so, if we have no detailed and accurate map based on the results of these voyages, it is because those who discovered a harbour or entry which had not been known before, and where they found inhabitants and were able to secure skins at a profit, availed themselves of the chance and concealed the news of their discovery, in the expectation that they would be able for a long while to carry on an exclusive trade in that district.

In the harbour we found the commandant of the department of San Blas, Don Juan de la Bodega y Quadra, captain in the navy, with the brigantine *Activo* alone of the vessels under his orders. On the thirteenth of June he had sent the frigate *Aransazu*, under the command of a naval lieutenant, Don Jacinto Caamaño, accompanied by several pilots, a designer and a map-drawer, to make an examination of the interior of the entry of Bucareli, and the frigate *Concepcion* to convey to the missions of San Francisco, Monterey and the Santa Barbara channel, the assistance annually sent to them at the expense of His Majesty.

There was also at Nootka the English frigate *Daedalus*, from Portsmouth, bringing supplies of food for the expedition of Captain Vancouver. Her commander, Thomas News, bore a royal order, sent by our minister of state, according to which the English officer who should deliver it to the commandant of this Spanish station was to be placed in possession of that which belonged to the English nation, under the terms of the convention concluded between the Spanish and British courts and signed at the royal residence of San Lorenzo, 28 October 1790. He had left England bearing this order, and Ricardo Augusto, lieutenant of the royal navy, carried the necessary instructions for the fulfilment of the order, and was commissioned to deliver these documents into the hands of Mr. Vancouver. But the sad fate which had befallen him in the Sandwich Islands, where he had fallen at the hands of the Indians, cut short the career of this worthy officer, whose merits had already gained for him an honourable reputation.

News of this event reached Captain Vancouver at a time when he was intending to continue for some while his explorations towards the north, and suspending them, he anchored at Nootka on 27 August. He told us that as he was coming out of the strait the two vessels under his command had grounded and had been on the point of being lost, to the south-west of Cape North, but he had succeeded in getting them off, the corvette being uninjured, while the brigantine was greatly damaged and it was necessary to overhaul her. He also informed us that he had explored the coast of the mainland as far as 52° 30′ north, and had found that from Cape North to the limit of his exploration the land was not so broken and did not contain so many entries as that part which lay farther south: he had only found one channel, which he entered for a short distance. The part of the coast which appears on our map as a dotted line is drawn from the copy which this officer communicated to us; he showed the same frankness and good faith as that with which we had informed him of our discoveries, from the account of which he took as much as he felt would be of service in completing his own map.

Captain Vancouver and Don Juan de la Bodega y Quadra, commandant of the department of San Blas, being commissioned by their respective courts to carry out the convention already mentioned, were not in agreement in their interpretation which was to be placed on the orders which they had received. Quadra said that in order to follow out the first article of this convention, it was necessary to settle what were the buildings, districts and portions of land mentioned in it, the clause reading: "That the officer of His Britannic Majesty who shall present this shall be placed in possession of the buildings, districts or portions of land which may have been occupied by subjects of that monarch in April 1789, as well on the harbour of Nootka as on the other harbour, which they said was called Port Cox, situated some seventeen leagues distant from the harbour first named, restoration being made to this officer of those things of which they have been dispossessed." In order to elucidate these points, Quadra had taken a deposition from Macuina, prince of the district, made in the presence of several impartial witnesses, and had sought information from the captain of the packet-boat *Feliz Aventurero*, Don Francisco Viana, from Mr. Ingram and from Robert Gray, who had been present at the events which had occurred at Nootka in the year 1789, on the occasion of the arrival of the Spanish frigate commanded by Don Estéban Joseph Martinez. As a result of all these inquiries, it appeared that Macuina had not sold or ceded any piece of territory to the English, and that they had only constructed on land a barrack of logs, which Captain Douglas had dismantled on his departure for the Sandwich Islands, and of which traces remained when Martinez arrived. On these grounds Quadra protested to the English commander that he could not make an unconditional delivery of the harbour of Nootka and of the territories which surrounded it, but that he agreed to cede the houses, workshops and plantations which we Spaniards had made and constructed with so much labour and care, retiring to the harbour of Nuñez Gaona at the entrance of Fuca Strait, until such time as the two courts, having received information from the commissioners whom they had appointed, should decide upon the means for bringing the matter to a conclusion.

To this proposal Vancouver replied by insisting on the delivery of the buildings, districts and portions of land which the vassals of H.B.M. had occupied in 1789, as well on the harbour of Nootka as on that which is known by the name of Port Cox. Quadra, however, would not agree that there had been such an occupation at that time, and as he was further assured that there had not then existed at Nootka houses, buildings or lands belonging to Englishmen and forming the alleged station of which the surrender and delivery was demanded, the two commissioners,

Spanish and British, agreed to leave matters as they were and to render an account to their respective courts of the grounds upon which they had reached this decision.

After our departure from the harbour, there had anchored there, in addition to the ships of Vancouver and the frigate *Daedalus*, the Portuguese packet-boat *Feliz Aventurero*, with a cargo of five hundred skins. She had sailed from Macao on 4 May 1791; in the entry of Prince William, she had lost a large part of her crew and necessity had compelled her to seek anchorage, her supplies being already exhausted. The brigantine *Venus*, Captain Henry Shepherd, from Bengal, had also arrived, as well as an American frigate, commanded by Mr. Gray; the American brigantine *Hope*, commanded by Mr. Ingram; the American frigate *Margaret*, Captain James Mage, commander of several vessels belonging to Boston; an English frigate of thirty guns, called the *Butterworth*, Captain William Brown, bringing letters for Vancouver and orders to form two stations on the coast and one on Queen Charlotte Island; the English sloop *Prince Leo*, commanded by Mr. Spar, of Brown & Company, who sailed from London in October 1791; the English brigantine *Tresbes*, commanded by William Alder, lieutenant, R.N., with letters for Vancouver; and a sloop in distress, for whose repair permission was asked from Don Jaun de la Bodega; he accorded it and further supplied whatever help he thought would be useful.

CHAPTER XVI

Nautical information and description of Nootka Sound and Island.—Products of the land and of the sea surrounding it.

Don Juan Perez, graded as an ensign of frigates, in command of the frigate *Santiago*, which had sailed from San Blas to explore the north-west coast of America, anchored in 1774 off Point San Esteban, which was afterwards called Rocky Point by Captain Cook. He entered into relations with the natives who appeared, and gave the place the name of San Lorenzo Harbour. In 1778 the said English captain visited the district, and being unaware that any foreigner had preceded him in making its discovery, he called the place King George's Harbour. Gathering afterwards that the Indians called it "Nootka," he adopted this name. The fact is, however, that no such word is known to the natives, the only sound like it in their language being "Nutchi," which means "mountain," and there is no indication that they have ever called this harbour anything except "Yucuatl."

The mouth of the harbour is two and a half miles wide. Within it, there are several small islands, of moderate altitude and covered with woods; on the eastern side lies the island of Nootka, so named by Quadra and Vancouver, of which the exact extent was not known accurately in 1781, when the corvettes *Descubierta* and *Atrevida* were there. The commander of these vessels dispatched Don Joseph de Espinosa and Don Ciriaco Cevallos, lieutenants of the navy, to ascertain whether the channel which was to be seen to the north-east communicated with the bay of Good Hope, and whether any of its branches extended for so considerable a distance to the north-east or east as to suggest that they might be a passage to the other sea. These officers found that the station was situated on an island, some twenty miles from east to west, being fifteen miles broad from north to south at one extremity and five at the other. They discovered that the waters of Nootka Sound joined those of Good Hope Bay, and that the main channel had some branches which ran for a short distance into the interior of that which appeared to be the mainland, on which were found the winter quarters of the natives. Such was the outcome of their examination and of the astronomical observations carried out by the launches of the corvettes during a period of eight days, in which time they navigated from east to west close to the coasts of this great gulf, regaining the open sea by Good Hope Bay and returning to the ships from which they had set out.

Viewed from the sea the island of Nootka presents a pleasing appearance at all times. Its high ground is covered with numerous pines and cypresses, which are evergreen, and which produce an impression of fertility and beauty which is dissipated as soon as any one sets foot on shore. Formed of a grey stone and covered for the most part with the mould formed by decaying trees and plants, it is skirted by poor beaches, by precipices and by barren tracts of land. The naturalist, Don Francisco Mosiño, asserts that there are some veins of metal in the hilly ground of this island, and he inclines to believe that there are veins of iron and copper and one of silver.

The harbour on the shores of which we established a station was named Friendly Cove by Cook and Santa Cruz by Don Estéban Martinez. It is a small bay almost blocked by an islet, on which stands the fort designed to protect the entrance. There is a good anchorage, and it is sufficiently near the land for ships to be moored to the shore. The tide at full moon and new moon is at its highest at twenty minutes past noon, and spring tide rises to fifteen feet.

From the beginning of May until the end of August, fine weather is enjoyed on most days; at midnight the wind blows from land or from the north-east, and this ceases at seven or eight in the morning. Between ten and eleven the wind blows from the north-west, being sometimes very strong; this continues until nightfall, when it falls and veers to the north. At the end of August, the winds are generally from the second and third quarters; the sky begins to be covered with cloud, and rains are frequent. The most severe storms and tempests are experienced in November, although it is only rarely that there is any thunder. The north winds are terrible in winter, and their force is such that they tear up trees by the roots and imperil any ships which are at the anchorage. It is not until January that it begins to freeze, and although the smaller channels are covered with ice, the navigation of the main channel is always open. In general, the climate of this country is much more temperate than that of the eastern shore of America at the same parallel.

The healthiness of the climate may be gathered from the small amount of illness among the natives and the fact that Europeans enjoyed excellent health during the period of our stay in the harbour. It is true that some members of the naval and military forces which were at the station on land suffered from fever and scurvy, but this was the outcome of the bad food which they consumed and of the constant drenchings to which they were exposed when engaged in felling timber in the woods.

Despite the fact that the rock is sparsely covered with earth, the land is not unfertile. It is very difficult to penetrate into the depth of the woods, both on account of the deep gullies which are found there and because they are almost closed by the thick growth of pines, cypresses, some cedars and oaks, many medicinal herbs, and other plants which have very sweet-smelling flowers and fruit with an agreeable taste. Of those plants which our compatriot, Don Pedro Alberni, captain of infantry, cultivated, all attained the same size and quality as those produced in the fertile lands of Andalusia. Only wheat and maize could never come to maturity; the plant grows vigorously, and the wheat became very tall, but no grain ever formed in the ear. Barley was cultivated with better success, and the land yielded potatoes in abundance. Despite this fertility, as the ground is covered with snow in the winter, and in summer enough grass cannot be grown to provide for the other seasons, it is not a suitable land for raising cattle or sheep, and it is only possible to keep a few head of goats or pigs.

The natives only inhabit the coasts, leaving the mountains to bears, deer, lynx, wolves, beavers, badgers, otters, squirrels, moles and rats. The rats which went ashore from European ships have increased so enormously that they cause serious damage in the stores and houses.

The land birds found in the district of Nootka are sparrows with a curved beak, woodpeckers, canaries, grey pigeons, herons, eagles with white heads and necks, crows and humming birds. The aquatic birds are not numerous, and there are found only some fresh- and salt-water ducks, diving-birds, curlew and gulls. Among reptiles, snakes and vipers have been seen. Of insects, those which are most troublesome are the mosquitoes, which are very plentiful, and from the bites of which the natives suffer greatly.

The sea which washes the shores of Nootka is richer, since it produces excellent salmon, ling, cod, eels, trout, soles, ray, sardines, herrings, etc. But of its diverse and valuable products, the Indians chiefly value two, the whale and the otter, the former because it provides them with food for much of the time, and the latter because with its skin they cover themselves and protect themselves, while it is also the only money or medium of exchange of which they make use in carrying on trade.

The sea-otter is an amphibious animal, but it lives almost continuously in the water, and it travels to a considerable distance from the shore. It can be seen sometimes far out to sea swimming rapidly, carrying its young at its breast, and at other times on its back, as long as they are unable to swim for themselves; in this way it goes from place to place, generally with no other object than to find the small fish which serve for its food. These animals have never been known to forsake their young, even when they see that they are in imminent danger of being caught, since, hampered by this care, they are unable to use all their agility; they always prefer to die rather than to leave their young and abandon them.

The luxury of Asiatics and the necessity and interest of the Indians have combined to destroy this valuable type of animal on the north-west coast of America, which is frequented by many foreign vessels for no other reason than that they may gather a cargo of the largest possible number of skins in order to sell them at Canton. The natives who wish to utilise the skins not only to supply themselves with the necessary clothing, but also in order to secure finery and to purchase copper and shells, which objects form the greater part of their wealth, hunt the otters with such energy that there is hardly a point on the coast, from the thirty-sixth to the sixtieth degree of latitude, the inhabitants of which do not engage in this pursuit during the summer. The constitution of the lungs of the otter, which does not allow it to remain under water for more than two or three minutes, is a great advantage for its pursuers, although the speed with which it swims often enables it to escape the sight even of those who are most dexterous in this form of hunting.

The beauty of the skin varies according to the age of the animal. When they are a few months old they are covered with a whitish fur which is ugly; this they presently lose, and there then appears another type of fur, short and dark. When the otter comes to its full growth it sheds this fur and becomes entirely black, and its skin is then at its most beautiful, but when this time is passed, it begins to deteriorate, and consequently its value decreases. The male is much more handsome than the female, the latter having her neck and belly covered with white fur which is not very thick. Experts agree in preferring otter skins which have very close fine hair, black and shiny, with silver strands here and there glistening on the neck and belly.

CHAPTER XVII

The inhabitants of Nootka.—Their complexion and physiognomy, their dress and ornaments, dwellings and food.—Idea that these natives were cannibals.—Entire absence of any evidence that they were so, in our experience.

We are indebted to our compatriot, Don Francisco Mosiño, for almost all the knowledge and information which we have regarding the natives of Nootka, with whom Mosiño had extended intercourse and dealings during the time in which he was with the naval captain, Don Juan de la Bodega y Quadra, and residing at Nootka in the capacity of naturalist attached to the expedition commanded by that officer in the summer of 1792. The discernment of this deserving man, his constancy, the intelligence which he displayed in acquiring the Nutkeño dialect, the intimate friendship which he formed with the most typical Indians and those who were the best informed among the dwellers in the native settlement, and his long residence there, are the grounds upon which our impartial judgment leads us to prefer the results of his inquiries to those of any inquiries which we ourselves made.

All the time during which we were at Nootka was employed in refitting our vessels, in astronomical observations and in those hydrographic labours which constituted the principal object of the commission entrusted to us. Accordingly we were unable to devote ourselves energetically to the study of the manners and customs of the natives of the country, and the public would be left without information of much interest if we did not present to it that which Don Francisco Mosiño acquired at the same time as that of our voyage.

Generally speaking, the Nutkeños are of medium build; their chiefs, however, are extremely fat. Their appearance is not different from that of the other Americans living on the mainland, except that the inhabitants of Nootka have heads which end in a point; they are undoubtedly born so, and it is not to be attributed to the fact that they are put in oblong chests, which serve them for beds, and that their heads are moulded with strong bandages which come down almost to the eyes. This practice produces no ill results, but it does seem to help to alter their appearance somewhat, raising the eyebrows and changing the horizontal position of the eyes. Many of those whom we met had a languid expression, but we found few who appeared to be devoid of intelligence; in most we observed a lively wit, which gave clear evidence of their quick understanding. It is rare not to find them with very prominent ankles and with their feet pointing somewhat inwards, which is probably the result of the way in which they pass their whole childhood with their feet bound up, and of the position which they occupy in their canoes. To the same cause may be attributed their clumsy way of walking and a kind of stiffness which is especially noticeable in their women. Their hair is long, flaccid and thick, varying in colour between red, dark chestnut and black. Young men begin to show beards at the same age as those of other lands, and in old age they have beards as thick and long as those of the Turks, but the young men are without beards, since they pull out the hairs with their fingers or more often with pincers made of small shells. The quantity of grease with which they anoint their bodies and the earths of different colours with which they paint themselves prevent their natural colour from being seen. From that which can be observed in the case of the children, however, it may be inferred that they are not so dark as the Mexicans, and if we may judge from the case of a daughter of the tais, who one day washed herself at our request, we should say that the Nutkeños are entirely white.

In childhood they are accustomed to make three or four holes in the lower part of their ears and one or two through their nostrils. In these last they to-day fix small pieces of copper, having given up the use of rings which served them for ornaments at the time when Captain Cook visited them in 1778. Through the holes pierced in their ears they pass three or four ear-rings, inserting one on top of another, without paying any regard to their order or size. They use necklaces made of small fish bones or of green shells and beads which they have secured by trading with Europeans. While they neglect the hair of their beards, they devote much attention to that on their heads, taking great pride in having it well-looking. Every one trims it according to his own taste; it is more usual for them to wear it loose and evenly parted, but some of them wear a band. They also surround their heads with chaplets formed of the fibre of cypress bark, and on festivals they wear in their hair many white feathers, taken from the smallest and finest ducks, eagles and herons, making use of whale grease, which they call "haca-miz," in place of pomade. With this grease they anoint their whole body, and afterwards paint themselves with a kind of varnish made from the same grease or oil, and from red ochre, in such a way that it seems to be their natural colour.

It is certainly a thing worthy of remark that man, revolting from the idea of appearing with the form and colour which he has received from Nature, almost always succeeds in disfiguring himself, and that in this respect he prefers his own caprices and whims to beauty itself. Although it is a general opinion that women of all times and of all lands are those who have most cultivated this pernicious art, and who have been guilty of the greatest extravagances in pursuing it, the contrary appears at Nootka. It can be observed that the women of this country do not mortify their flesh by cutting it, and they do not pull their ears out of shape by the weight of metal ornaments, as do the men. This peculiarity is the more remarkable since their neighbours who live on Queen Charlotte Island make a horrible slash across their faces in order to fix there one of the chief ornaments. It may be that the women of Nootka are surer of being able to attract the attention of their men, an idea to which colour is lent by the fact that the number of women is very small in proportion to that of the male inhabitants.

The Nutkeños are not content with disfiguring themselves in the manner described, but they are also in the habit of wearing masks, on which are painted horrible heads of men and animals. The taises distinguish themselves in this as in other forms of disfigurement, and they can never be confused with the common people, who are permitted to paint themselves with one colour only, it being the prerogative of the chiefs also to have their eyelids painted and to have various figures and drawings on their faces.

The dress of the natives of Nootka is very simple, merely consisting in the case of the men of a mantle or square cape, made of the fibre which they procure from cypress bark, and which they combine with the hair of wild goats. It must be understood that this cloak does not suffice to cover their nakedness, and certainly they often throw it aside, and appear stark naked even in the largest gatherings of people. The women, on the contrary, are very modest, and under a cloak similar to that worn by the men, they wear a kind of under garment, tied to the body at the waist, which covers them completely. Men are also seen wearing bearskins, the largest and blackest that they can find, and these with otter skins constitute a dress of which the use is confined to nobles and other persons of position. Macuina was in the habit of wearing an excellent cloak of very fine otter skins, woven together with such skill that it was necessary to examine it with great care in order to find at the back the threads which joined the skins to each other. This same chief occasionally appeared with an exquisite cloak of weasel skins, and on other occasions wore also deerskins very well tanned.

To protect their heads from the rays of the sun, these islanders wear a cap of badger skin, or more often hats made of very flexible grass or reeds, of a white colour, on which they draw designs or set ornaments. These always form part of the equipment of the whalers; those of the common people are marked by their inferior quality, or, more generally, by the fact they have no designs and ornaments.

In time of war they wear a special covering made of leather, prepared from the hides of deer, which differ only from those which our soldiers use in the interior provinces of Mexico in the fact that they are larger. These leather jackets protect them from arrows, which cannot generally pierce them; they are not easily pierced with a spear.

The weapons of these natives consist of spears five yards long, with a point of copper, iron or shell, which are generally a finger's length; they have small bows which are little flexible and arrows which are very badly fashioned. They now are able to use firearms and European swords extremely well; among the inhabitants of Nootka we found some who used muskets with skill and safety, and who were able to load and unload intelligently both muskets and pistols. One form of work in which they clearly show intelligence is in the construction of their houses, and perhaps Europeans themselves, with all the advantages which they have in the matter of mechanical knowledge, would find it difficult to do the same work with the scanty materials that the Nutkeños have for labour of such importance. They made the walls of planks, very large, placed upright, one overlapping the other, and strongly fastened to some stakes or feet driven into the ground and serving as a foundation. On huge pillars of pinewood, placed in the middle of the space which forms the dwelling, rests an enormous beam which serves to support the planks which form the roof. Other beams, of smaller size, serve the same purpose, but the planks are left unfastened, so that they can be brought together or separated, according as may be determined in order to regulate the light, to let out smoke, or to serve other ends.

On the pillars which support the central beam, human faces are carved; these faces are deformed by their exaggerated size and by the ugliness of their expression, and to them the Indians give the name "Tlama." Captain Cook supposed that these figures represented the national gods, but was soon undeceived on finding that they were held in little esteem, the natives being ready to barter them for some iron or copper. The natives themselves told us that they were merely intended as an ornament, and that if there was in them any meaning, it was merely some allusion to the man whose strength had assisted to raise the timber to the place where it was and fix it there. The interior of these houses everywhere conveys an impression of poverty, disorder and dirt.

Set in the place of honour, we saw in the house of Macuina an oblong chest, a little more than two yards long and half a yard wide, on the inside of which there was painted a monstrous figure, with a most hideous human face, enormously large arms, nails like an eagle's talons, and feet like those of a bear. This chest seemed to be a kind of oratory for the chief of the tribe, and its singularity has induced us to give a drawing of it with the other pictures which illustrate the account of this voyage.

Their cooking utensils are all of wood and are few in number. The shell called sea-ear, which is found on the beaches of Monterey and in New Zealand, is the most luxurious vessel known in this land. The natives draw their chief food from the sea, and whether it is that it is not in sufficient quantity or whether they do not employ enough diligence in getting it, it is certain that they suffer great famines. Being entirely without salt, they preserve the fish by drying it in smoke, and at their meals whale oil or sardine oil serves as their only condiment. They also make use of venison, and do not despise the flesh of bears and otters. They are fond of the flesh of geese, ducks and other aquatic birds, but it could not be discovered if they employed the flesh of eagles in the same way or whether they hunted them solely for the sake of their feathers. On one occasion a prince referred to the number of dishes with which Macuina was in the habit of entertaining other taises who came to visit him, and he related that there were as many as thirty-six different forms of food. Intercourse with us has made them fond of bread, chocolate and other European foods, and this to such an extent that beans cooked in the manner of New Spain are called by them "Tays-frixoles," that is, "the dish of kings."

There seems to be no doubt that these savages were once cannibals, imitating the barbarous custom of the natives of New Zealand and of other Pacific islands. There is great ground for believing this from the fact that they brought to sell to the ships of Captain Cook a skull and the bones of a hand with some flesh sticking to them; to the packet-boat *San Carlos*, under the command of Eliza, they brought the roasted hand of a child, and they brought other parts of the body, prepared in the same way, to other ships. It is also true that when this point was discussed with them, they did not deny that this detestable practice had existed among some of their chiefs. Prince Hau-itl assured us that it was not every one who had eaten human flesh, and that they had not eaten

Praying-room of Macuina.

it constantly, but that only the most valiant warriors did so when they were preparing to go to battle.

The English captain Meares relates that when coming on board his ship, Macuina received a blow on one foot, and while the surgeon came to attend to it, he sucked the blood that flowed from the wound. The surgeon expressed disapproval of this, but Macuina answered, smiling, "Good, good," and confessed that he ate human flesh and that he delighted to feast on it.

Caliquen and Hanapa assured the same Captain Meares of the aversion which they had for this form of food, but at the same time they confessed that the custom of eating human flesh existed among them, adding that every moon Macuina killed a slave to satisfy his barbarous appetite. They gave the following account of the manner in which this bloody ceremony was performed.

The number of slaves owned by Macuina is very considerable, not only in Nootka but also in other parts of that district. When the fatal day set apart for the feast upon the human victim arrived, a certain number of these slaves were caused to assemble at the house of the sovereign chief, and the one upon whom the lot fell had to be eaten at the entertainment which immediately followed. The inferior chiefs invited to share in the banquet were the ministers who performed the preliminary ceremonies. Their duty was to intone martial songs, to dance round the fire, and to feed the flames by pouring oil upon them. Presently they looked at Macuina, and he, with his accustomed skill, had to catch a slave. The activity of the chief in chasing these wretches, and their eagerness to escape from his fierce clutch, constituted the most interesting part of the horrible spectacle. But it rarely occupied much time; the one who had the misfortune to fall into the hands of the destroyer was at once put to death, and his body, cut in slices, was distributed to the guests, while those who had been happy enough to avoid such imminent danger showed their delight with shouts and other expressions of joy.

From the time at which our station was established at Nootka, there had been no example of a repetition of such inhuman sacrifices, whether on account of the fact that so atrocious a custom was abominated by Europeans and vigorously opposed by them, or because it was necessary to select the victims from among prisoners made in war, and hence the peace which the Nutkeños had enjoyed since 1789 had been an obstacle.

CHAPTER XVIII

Continuation of the information gained concerning the manners and customs of the inhabitants of Nootka.—Arts on which the natives of both sexes employ themselves.—Government, religion, funeral rites and other practices which seem to be connected with the creed of these peoples.

A PEOPLE that lives by fishing cannot find possessions except on the shores and in the seas by which those shores are washed, and thus the inhabitants of this archipelago dispute in arms for the right to fish in the areas which respectively belong to them, regarding it as an infringement of public law if their waters are invaded by foreigners for the purpose of fishing. As it is from the sea that they derive their main support, they live always near the coast and they change their place of residence as the fish remove from one part to another. At Cape Frondoso begin the migratory settlements of Macuina, separated from each other by a distance of two or three miles. The government of some of these settlements is in the hands of one of his brothers, the government of others in the hands of one of his wives. When winter comes on, they remove their settlements to more sheltered positions: those at Cape Frondoso are removed to the neighbourhood of Macuina Point; those which were situated there to Marvinas, and these to Copti; and all are eventually removed to Tasis, where the severe months of December and January are spent. The greater number of these scattered bodies or people being at last collected together, the inhabitants support existence on the store of fish which has been collected in the previous months. The Mischimis pass the nights singing and dancing round their fires, giving themselves up to every licentious excess, and their taises receive at Tasis the visits of their friends and allies the Nuchimases, and those of other neighbouring nations who come to pay their respects.

The small number of the inhabitants of Yucuatl and the simplicity of their manner of life does not permit them to number among them many artisans, nor does it allow any great variation in their forms of employment and duties. The men work at carpentry, are fishermen and hunters, and the women employ themselves mainly in sewing and weaving; but all learn to attain excellence in the special art or employment in which they engage, so far as knowledge of these various occupations extends in that country. The construction of their canoes is the art in which these natives display most ingenuity, for without instruments for the purpose they build them so exactly proportioned that they are extremely light and strong and very well shaped. Men and women alike manage these canoes well in the sea; they are skilled in the use of oars, which they use also to steer the boats, since none of them have rudders. When a canoe is sighted at a distance, although the costume of both sexes appears to be the same when far off, it is possible to know whether men or women are in it, because the paddles used by the latter are blunt at the end and those used by the men are pointed, which enables them to wound their enemies in a naval combat.

Fishing is a form of industry to which necessity obliges them to devote themselves, both in order to know where each kind of fish can be found in abundance, and the method which must be employed to catch them. They formerly used fish-hooks of wood and shell, made with considerable art, but they now only use iron hooks. Their nets are small and are of use only for taking very small fish. Sardine fishing, where that kind of fish is most plentiful, also offers much amusement; to carry it on, several canoes come together and occupy at the mouth of the harbour all the passages by which the fish might be able to escape. They then shake long poles under the water in order to frighten the fish, and the canoes, which lie in a circle, gradually come nearer to each other; the circle thus becomes continually smaller, until they have collected the fish in a small space, from which they draw them with great speed, using nets, small cans, jars and other means. When the work is done, the chief distributes the fish equally and in an ordered manner to the various settlements.

Still more ingenious is their method for capturing whales. A very small canoe, which is sometimes fifteen feet long and two and a half broad, managed by three or four men, is the vessel which sets out to take the most enormous animal of all those which Nature produces. They throw with force at the whale a sharp harpoon, fastened to a long and sufficiently heavy stake, so that it pierces the animal deeply. A rope attached to one end of the harpoon is fastened to a bladder which floats on the water and acts as a buoy: this indicates the course followed by the wounded animal during the short time for which it continues to live. The skill and daring needed if the shot is not to be misdirected, and in order to surmount the dangers of this form of fishing, are points which will appeal at once to those who have any practical experience. Quatlazapé, a brother of Macuina, prided himself on being a master of this art, which is indeed that form of fishing to which the natives attach the greatest importance and from which they derive the greatest advantages. The same chief was accustomed to preside over the distribution of the prey, and when this had been done, to give a magnificent banquet to those who had gathered from all the villages, whom he treated with remarkable courtesy.

Otter hunting is difficult and demands much agility and skill in those who take part in it. Generally two canoes set out together, with two men in each, equipped with bows and arrows and with a small harpoon, to which is attached a fairly long cord; this is employed to draw the animal in when it has been wounded, and to bring it alongside. They sometimes surprise an otter sleeping on the water, and if they have the good fortune to come near it before it disappears, then, when they drag it alongside, a fierce struggle takes place between the hunters and their prey, whose teeth are sufficiently formidable. The more usual method of catching the otter, however, is to chase it when it has been sighted at a suitable distance. The characteristic of these animals which prevents them from remaining long under water and which compels them to show themselves from time to time, reveals the course which they are following to their pursuers. When they come within range, the Indians attack the animal with arrows and harpoons, but its speed often enables it to elude the watchfulness and to exhaust the breath of its enemies. This does not occur when the otter is carrying its young, which male and female alike defend with the greatest ferocity, breaking the arrows and harpoons in pieces with their teeth, although in the end they become the prey of their pursuers, and die, still shielding and protecting their little ones.

The Nutkeña women are mainly engaged in the sedentary occupations of spinning and weaving. They have no distaffs except their teeth and fingers, with which they bind together cypress fibre and otter hair in order to form a thick plait. This they then make thinner and longer, until they have a skein about a foot long. They use the most simple looms, making a warp out of a cane set horizontally at a height of four and a half feet from the ground; they move their fingers along it rapidly in different directions and with extraordinary skill, making up in this way for the lack of tools which would in any other case be necessary and indispensable for this work.

The government of these natives may be described as patriarchal, since the chief of the nation fulfils at one and the same time the functions of father of the family, king and high priest. The vassals receive their support from the hand of the monarch or chief whom they represent in those villages which are far from the court, and they believe that they owe this benefit to the intercession of their sovereign with the supreme being. There is in Nootka no intermediate grade between princes and slaves; all are slaves except such as are the brothers or very near relatives of the tais. The slaves are known by the name of Mischimis, which was that of the first Tays-Kalari, that is "brothers of the chief." The effects of this superiority and absolute dominion are, however, mitigated by the fact that the tais is convinced that his prayers would not in themselves suffice to maintain his sovereignty and to supply the means of subsistence to his subjects, and that it is therefore necessary to make use also of their labour in fishing and hunting and in other necessary activities.

The belief and religion of these inhabitants has in it much that is curious. They recognise the existence of a God who is the creator and preserver of all things, and they believe also in another malignant being, the author of wars, of illnesses and death. They abominate and detest this hateful origin of their misfortunes, while they venerate and praise the good God who created them. In His honour the chief fasts for many days and preserves inviolable chastity and purity whenever it is not full moon. Accompanied by his household, he sings hymns in celebration of the blessings received from Quautz, as they call the Creator, and as a thanksgiving for His goodness the chief throws whale grease on the flames and scatters feathers to the winds.

The Nutkeños say that the propagation of the human race was brought about in the following manner. God created a woman, whom He left alone in the dark forests of Yucuatl, where there lived also deer without horns, dogs without tails and geese without wings. The woman lamented her sad situation day and night without finding any solace, until Quautz took pity on her tears, and appeared to her, coming over the waters in a canoe of copper, which shone brightly, in which many handsome young men were rowing with oars of the same metal. The island maiden was astonished at this sight and remained dumbfounded by the foot of a tree. One of the rowers, however, told her that it was the Almighty who had had the goodness to visit these shores and to supply her with that companionship for which she sighed. At these words the sad and desolate maiden cried the more, and as the tears trickled down her nostrils, the moisture fell from them to the sand. Quautz then commanded her to look at that which had fallen, and she saw with amazement the tiny body of a child which was entirely formed. By order of Quautz, she placed this in a shell suitable for its size, being told to move the child to other shells as it grew larger. When this work had been completed, the Creator re-embarked, after having allowed the brute beasts also to experience His bounty, for at the same moment the deer beheld horns sprouting from his forehead, the dog found a tail growing, and the birds rose in the air to make trial for the first time of those wings which they had now received. The new-born babe gradually grew, being moved from cradle to cradle until it began to walk. It proved to be a boy, and the first proof which he gave of his manhood was that his mistress conceived by him. Her first-born son is the ancestor of the taises, while from her other sons the common people are descended.

It is difficult to know what to say of a certain Marlox, an inhabitant of the highlands, for whom all have an overmastering terror. They describe his shape as monstrous, entirely covered with thick and coarse black hair; his head is like that of a man, but his teeth are very long, sharp and strong as those of a bear; his arms are very huge, and his fingers and toes end in long curved nails. His shouts fell any one who hears them to the ground, and any wretch upon whom his blow falls is shattered into a thousand pieces.

The Nutkeños believe that the soul of man is immortal and that after death it passes to another life. There is, however, this distinction, that the souls of taises and of princes nearly related to them go to join the souls of their ancestors in the residence of Quautz, and the souls of the common people or Mischimis go to another place called Pin-pula, the lord of which is Izmitz. Those who are with Quautz are the authors of lightning and rain, the first being a sign of their displeasure and the latter of their goodwill. When any misfortune befalls a tais, rain is the tears which his compassionate ancestors shed from heaven, and lightning the arrows which they hurl down to punish the wrongdoers. Such taises as are given to lasciviousness, such as are gluttons, as neglect to offer sacrifices, and as are slack or careless in prayer, suffer at their death the miserable fate of the common herd.

The distinction which they draw between the lot of the people generally and that of the princes appears in their funeral rites. The corpses of taises and other princes are carried with much pomp and continual lamentation on the part of the Mischimis to the slopes of Conuma, a very lofty mountain; they are then placed on couches thickly covered with exquisite otter skins in a wooden chest, which they hang from the branches of a tree. This ceremony is attended by some of their friends from allied nations, such as the Nuchimases, and they dip their fingers in the blood which flows from cuts made in various parts of the body, but generally on the breast. Four or six of those who were servants of the dead man spend every day in watching the corpse, and upon them is laid the duty of singing various funeral hymns round the tree; they say that the soul still watches them, and that it does not abandon the body in which it dwelt until it is entirely decayed. The Mischimis are buried in the earth, so that they may be nearer the house in which Izmitz dwells. No suffering is involved for them in their fate, unless it be regarded as suffering for them to see themselves for ever parted from their former lords and unable ever to rise to the surface of that land in which they lived. The taises do not believe this recompense unjust, since it seems to be rather the result of the blind accident of birth than of any personal merit or demerit in the individuals; they take into consideration the fact that the common people can at all times enjoy the delights of sensuality, not being bound to the rigorous observance of fasts, or to the labour which is involved in offering prayers and performing acts of merit, all of which weigh heavily on the chiefs. The common people are therefore unworthy of a reward which could in any way bring them to be akin to the Deity. The death of a tais is mourned for four months; the outward signs of grief consist only in cutting the hair of the women until it reaches only four or six inches below the ears. The belief that the actually reigning monarch will in due time pass to be one of the blessed in whose power it is to direct at their will all the elements of heaven, obliges his subjects to treat him with the reverence due to a sacred personage. It is not permitted to touch the sovereign even accidentally; in proof of this may be cited the case in which one of our officers, having happened to throw some small pebbles at Macuina, trusting to the excellent terms on which he was with that chief, a venerable old man came up to him and, turning aside his hand, said to him: "One does not jest thus with a tais."

The dignity of tais is hereditary, descending from father to son, and regularly passes to the son if the father, owing to age or other causes, cannot continue to govern. During our stay at Nootka in 1792, there were there three principal taises, the chief of them all being Macuina on many grounds. His father fell in 1778 in war against the Thahumases, a nation of the situation of whose country we are ignorant, but which, judging from the etymology of the name, must lie on the other side of the sea, although the direction and distance cannot be determined. His son and successor avenged his death, going in person to the settlements of the enemy, where he did horrible slaughter. Quicomasia and Tiupananulg are the other two chiefs, whose fathers were still alive, but who retained only their priestly dignity, either because that dignity was not believed to be alienable or because age increased in them their love of religion. The most common form of conversation among these taises is boasting of things which seem to them to exalt them above others. Quicomasia said that he was greater than Macuina because he was tais of the Nuchinas and tais of Nootka. The brothers of the tais constitute the second rank of the nobility, but they lose this dignity at the end of two or three generations, since relations beyond the third degree do not share in it, but fall immediately into the class of the Mischimis, or plebeians. Women take the status of their fathers and husbands.

Polygamy is established among the taises and the princes, "kalati." It seems that they regard it as a sign of grandeur to pay and keep several women, although on one occasion a prince told us that three wives was the number necessary to have in order that intercourse with a wife who was pregnant might be avoided. The acquisition of a wife is very costly for the taises, since they cannot obtain them from the hands of their fathers except at the price of many sheets of copper, otter skins, shells, cypress fibre and fishing canoes. The result is that he who has five or six daughters who are good-looking regards them as means by which he may become extremely rich. For the Mischimis, it is almost always impossible to go to such expense, since, as they own no more than a small part of the fruit of their labour, they are never able to collect the dower; many of them, therefore, die unmarried. Such as have better fortune content themselves with a single woman, whom they receive as a gift from their lords in reward for their service.

The marriage ceremonies of the Nutkeños consist simply in an entertainment which the friends of the families of the newly married couple supply. The women are fertile, not being in this respect essentially different from European women. We do not know whether they assist childbirth by any means, but they certainly do not suffer the acute pain experienced by our women on such occasions, since, as soon as they have been delivered, they go to the sea and swim for a long while entirely naked. A curious fact is that as soon as a child is born, if its father be a tais, it is shut up in the hut and is not allowed to see the sun or the waves of the sea, for fear that Quautz might be deeply offended and kill both father and son. When the infant is a month old, all the nobles assemble and give it a first name, the allegorical meaning of which either refers to its own father or to some other person. The new name is celebrated with feasts and other expressions of delight, at which the tais makes presents of otter skins, copper and any ornaments that he can give to the nobles who have come to congratulate him. The names of the child are changed at different ages, and each alteration of this kind is celebrated with greater luxury and magnificence than the last. The young tais who, at the time of our first visit to Nootka in 1792, was called Quicsioconuc, was called Tlupaniapa in his infancy, Namajamitz when he reached the age of puberty, Gugumetazautlz in his early manhood, and finally Quicomasia, having enjoyed the privileges of manly age from the time when he entered into possession of the dignity of a tais. His last name meant "Extremely liberal prince." That of his father, Anape, signified, "Chief who towers over others as a tall pine tree over the small"; the name Macuina means "Tais of the sun."

As soon as the first signs of puberty appear in a woman, great feasts are given on this account, and her name is also changed; on the same day they are declared to be princesses, if they happen to be daughters of the principal chief of all the taises. The officers from our station went to congratulate Macuina on the installation of his daughter Istocoti-Clemoc, who had been previously called Apenas. The pomp which dignified this occasion is worthy of description. At one corner of the house, which was placed on the slopes of the woody mountains of Copti, they had set up a platform supported by four thick pillars, painted white, yellow, scarlet, blue and black, with various badly drawn figures on them, and two busts at the corners with opened arms and hands stretched out as if to signify the munificence of the monarch. In the interior of the house, on some freshly strewn rushes, there was a couch, where the young princess lay, dressed in the finest cypress threads and loaded with innumerable ornaments. As soon as the appointed hour arrived, Macuina took his daughter by the hand and led her to a platform, placing her on his right and Quatlaza-pé on his left. The large crowd of natives who thronged the hall and beach remained in the most profound silence. Then the chief, addressing them all, said: "My daughter Apenas is now no longer a girl but a woman; from this time forward she will be known by the name Istocoti-Clemoc," that is, "the great princess of Yucuatl." To this all replied with loud shouts of "Huacas, Huacas, Macuina! Huacas, Istocoti-Clemoc!"—cries equivalent to our "Viva"; the greatest praise among these people is to express friendship, which is signified by the word "Huacas." The taises and the other nobles then began to sing and dance, every one receiving some gift of importance, which Quatlaza-pé scattered from the platform in the name of Macuina and of the princess.

One of the games which was played at this celebration was wrestling, the sands being the arena in which this struggle took place. A shell was the prize accorded to the victor, and twenty or thirty competitors, stark naked, appeared to contest the honour of the victory. Quatlaza-pé threw among them from above a small wooden cylinder, upon which the competitors tried to lay hands, snatching it one from the other, using every effort to get hold of it and to keep it, until the strongest or cleverest triumphed. The Spanish sailors took part in this battle, and the reward which they secured was always superior to that of the natives, since to the latter only shells were given, but to the former excellent otter skins. Macuina was greatly pleased that we had been present at this festivity, and at the end commanded Istocoti-Clemoc to come down from the platform, and leading her to one of the looms which happened to be in the best position in the house, said to her: "You are now a woman, my daughter, and you must not any longer spend your time except on performing the duties belonging to your sex." The girl, docile and obedient to the commands of her father, abandoning entirely the amusements of childhood, began to spin and weave. She had previously come every day to see us, singing, dancing and laughing, but from this time she surprised all by the gravity with which she behaved, taking no notice of greetings save by a slight inclination of her head, and being never able to laugh or to do more than utter one or two words. The commandant of the station enjoyed the friendship of Macuina to a very great degree; nevertheless, his requests did not avail to induce the chief to bring his daughter even once to dine with the officers, and whenever the subject was mentioned to him, he always replied that his daughter was a woman and must not leave the house.

A tais may not have intercourse with one of his wives except when the moon is at full, and even then he is bound to abstain from the pleasures of marriage if public misfortunes demand that he should fast and pray. On such occasions he goes, escorted by two or three of his servants, to the place appointed for the offering of prayer, and lying on his back with his hands on his breast remains for many hours in this position. At the end of this time he gets up and cries aloud, imploring the divine pity, frequently addressing his prayers to the dead taises, whose origin proves that they cannot be indifferent and whose goodwill he longs always to preserve, in order to win happiness through their protection. In this manner two or three days are spent, during which time he takes no other food than some herbs and a small amount of water every twenty-four hours. At other times he offers prayers within his own house in order to conjure away the storms which hinder the Mischimis in their fishing and other work. He is then shut up in the chest of which mention has already been made and strikes the boards sharply while he intones his prayers in a loud voice. One prayer which could be understood ran roughly as follows: "Give us good weather, O Lord, give us life; do not permit us to perish; turn thine eyes upon us; drive away the storms from the land

and take sickness from the inhabitants thereof; diminish the frequency of the rainstorms; permit us to behold bright days and clear skies." After this the tais remains in deep silence; the women gather near his tabernacle, calling him repeatedly by his name and offering him things to eat. He, however, is deaf to their importunity, and if by chance he opens his lips, it is only to pray with renewed fervour, the vehemence of his devout enthusiasm constantly increasing.

It was not possible to ascertain the reason or origin of a barbarous ceremony, the performance of which is reserved for the most valiant prince. It consists in this prince going in company with two Mischimis to the shore of a deep lake, on the banks of which he leaves his cloak in the care of his attendants, and, taking in each hand two pieces of the roughest pine bark, he hurls himself head downwards from a rock. Lifting his face above the waters after a little while, he rubs his two cheeks, forehead and chin violently with the two pieces of bark; he then dives again and repeats the same cruel performance as many times as he thinks proper, losing blood meanwhile, which flows freely from the wounded parts. The spectators encourage him with constant applause as long as this severe penance lasts. Quatlaza-pé did this in our sight, and the acclamations with which the natives applauded his pious daring consisted in the words, incessantly repeated by the Mischimis; "Huaichacus Quatlaza-pé," that is to say, "Quatlaza-pé is a worthy man."

CHAPTER XIX

Continuation of the account of the Nutkeños.—Their civil and criminal administration.—Evils introduced among them by Europeans.—Language of these natives; their method of counting and of reckoning time, etc.

WE have been able to obtain very little information concerning the civil and criminal administration established among these islanders. It would, however, appear that the former is purely economic and that the latter is in general arbitrary, while it may be remarked that the nobles enjoy such high consideration in Nootka that the taises do not dare even to reprove them verbally. Since vices increase as needs multiply, and as the needs of a people are proportionate to the standard of living prevailing among them, it follows that the vices of these savages are few in comparison with those which are found among our own people. In Nootka theft is unknown, for necessities are few in number and common to all, while it is also the case that as these natives are very obliging and very abstemious, they can procure whatever they require with the utmost readiness from the house of the tais. Trade with Europeans has brought to them knowledge of many things of which they had better have remained in ignorance, thereby preserving the original simplicity of their manners. Copper, which they hold in the same esteem as we do gold, has begun to introduce among the Nutkeños those ills which are born of greed; it is a fact that Macuina has been obliged to punish theft with the death penalty. The natives are already beginning to experience the terrible ravages of syphilis, which threatens them with the appalling fate which overtook the ancient inhabitants of California, a race which has become almost extinct owing to this disease. As the total population of Nootka does not exceed two thousand persons, it may be gathered that in a few years they will have for the most part perished, and that the political existence of the tribe which we are describing will have come to an end.

The language of these natives is at once the rudest and harshest that we have ever heard. Its words contain many consonants; the combinations -*tl* and -*tz*, when occurring in the middle or at the end of a word, are very strongly pronounced.

The natives count in tens, every number up to ten having a distinct name. "Twenty" is expressed as "twice ten," "thirty" by "three times ten," and so on. As it is very rarely that they have any need to make use of very large numbers, when it is necessary for them to do so they repeat five, six, seven and more times the word *ayó*, which signifies "ten." The unit of length is an extended hand or the breadth of a hand between an extended thumb and little finger, and they also indicate fractions in a similar manner, representing them by the breadth of one or more fingers.

Since eloquence has always been the daughter of strong passions, and since strong passions can fire the imagination even of savages, it is not strange if we assert that eloquent men are to be found among the Nutkeños, and as evidence of this we will give in full a speech made by Macuina, in order to satisfy our commandant, Don Juan de la Bodega y Quadra, in the matter of a crime with the commission of which the tais was unjustly charged.

In the depth of the woods was found the body of a young boy, covered with wounds, naked and with all the flesh torn from his calves; near the corpse were a scarf and an English clasp-knife stained with blood. It was thought by many that the Indians of Macuina, perhaps at the instigation of their chief himself, had committed this murder in order to secure the clothes and flesh of the unhappy victim. This report spread through all the foreign vessels which were then in the harbour, and their various captains promised to join with our people to avenge this atrocious crime. Ingram, the Boston captain, actually seized two servants of Macuina, called Frijoles and Agustin, on the following day, sending word to us and asking for a guard to carry them off to be confined on board our war brigantine the *Activo*. Terrified at the appearance of the guard, the prisoners threw themselves into the water, where, despite their dexterity in swimming, they were captured by our launch and carried in it, with their arms bound, before Don Juan de la Bodega y Quadra. The commandant was perfectly satisfied that they were innocent, since they had not been for a moment absent from our house on the night on which the murder was committed, and he accordingly released them, telling them to ask Macuina on his behalf to inquire who was the guilty person.

Two days later the chief appeared and addressed the commandant almost in the following words: "Frijoles and Agustin have told me that Ingram held them on his ship in order to deliver them over to the Mischimis of Spain, who carry muskets to slay any one who tries to escape from the fetters in which they are to be bound, that they may be placed in the prison which you have on board your vessel, but that you, knowing that they were falsely accused of this crime, ordered their release and allowed them to go free to Tasis, and that your own Mischimis told mine, as they were going, that I had instigated this evil deed. I do not believe that you think this; I believe that you will have considered that Macuina has a thousand reasons for being your friend. You have given me copper; from you I have received many shells to distribute at the celebration of the recognition of Apenas as a princess; yours were the cloth, the beads, the jacket, the iron tools, the glass and many other things with which I am provided; our mutual trust has reached the point that we have both slept in the same room, on which occasion, since you were unarmed and had no men by you to defend you, I could have taken your life, if a friend were capable of such treachery. You know me and you know my invariable conduct sufficiently well for you not to imagine that I should command that our friendship should be broken in order to slay a boy less able to defend himself than if he had been a woman. Do you not understand that a chief, such as I am, would enter upon war by slaying other chiefs and by opposing to your Mischimis the might of my own subjects? If we were enemies, your life is that which would be the first to be in deadly peril; know well that Wicananish has many muskets, has much powder, has many balls; know well that chief Hana has no small store and that as his men, like the Nuchimases, are my relations and allies; all of us joined together would form a far more numerous army than that of the Spaniards, English and Americans together, so that we should have no fear of entering into battle. Have not your brothers"—for so he called the Spanish officers—"often been alone in my house, as well as in those of Quicomasia and Nanaquius, well dressed, with watches and other curious adornments? What ill have they suffered? Which of my people has done any wrong to them? Have not you yourself gone out with no more than a small escort and found only that my subjects have surrounded you in their multitude for no purpose but to give lively expression to their friendship for you? How then can you allow your people to speak so unworthily of me? How can you allow Ingram to declare that Frijoles and Agustin murdered this boy? Make it known to all that Macuina is your true friend, that he is so far from wishing to injure the Spaniards, that he is ever ready to avenge any wrong done to them, such as that which they have, as I think, now received at the hands of the perfidious men of Iticoac. You already know the strength and daring of my brother Quatlaza-pé and of my relative Natzapé. If you will lend me your launch with four or six small cannon, I will command these two, with the most valiant of my Mischimis, to destroy those bandits and to purify the opposite shore. You may place on board such of your men as you will, that they and my people, no less than our enemies, may know that Macuina is one with Quadra and that Quadra is one with Macuina."

All the natives are generally fond of singing; their voices are naturally harmonious; they compass the whole octave, and the voices of the singers are accompanied by striking boards with any implement that happens to be at hand and by beating some small hollow vessels of which the sound is similar to that of the ayacastles of the Mexicans. One man generally gives them the note, and the rest follow him, varying their voices almost as is the case in chanting in our churches. One of the musicians at intervals ceases to play and shouts loudly, giving an epitome of the subject of the song. These songs are mostly hymns celebrating the goodness of Quautz, the generosity of friends and the excellence of their allies.

But these natives have not been able to refrain from revealing the fact that civilisation has not made them sensible of the softer notes of music and has not inclined them to attend to its ingenious and agreeable variations. They have no liking for it when it is soft, since it then fails to stir their imagination and to rouse their passions; when it is not loud, it has in it nothing to appeal to their simple mentality. Another chief, Nanaquius, despised our trills and all music in which the sweet languor of lower notes was predominant, saying that a man who trilled seemed to him to be shaking with cold, and that another man sang as if he were falling asleep.

While the chiefs make use of poetry and music only in order to praise their God and to celebrate the distinguished actions of their heroes, the common people indulge in more profane singing. One night they gave us an exhibition which certainly surpassed in its indecency any ancient Greek and Roman entertainment, and we found that it is in this type of amusement that they spend every winter night in Tasis, the taises themselves being often spectators at entertainments so obscene that they will not take part in the ribald songs, although they have no objection to hearing them.

Their dances are not numerous and have no plan or order. At the martial dance they appear armed with bows, arrows and muskets; the music is then more than usually raucous, while their expressions and actions are indicative merely of ferocity. They sometimes dress themselves up in the skins and heads of bears and deer, wearing then wooden masks which represent in an exaggerated form the appearance of some aquatic birds, the movements of which they attempt to imitate, as well as those of a hunter who is stalking. A bear falling into a net and his death, or the death of a deer pierced to the heart by an arrow, is represented so naturally and with music so suitable, that it cannot fail to excite admiration. Decency compels us to pass over in silence the obscene dances of the Mischimis, especially that which represents a man become impotent through old age and that which represents an unhappy man who has never been able to marry. The women dance awkwardly; they rarely indulge in this form of amusement, and never except in the presence of those with whom they have first become very intimate.

The chronology of the Nutkeños is full of obscurity. The coming of Quautz in the copper canoe is the epoch at which they begin to count the years, but as the number of months in a year and that of the intercalary days is differently reckoned, it is impossible to make any exact comparison with our calendar. The difficulty is increased by the fact that a large number of days and months is vaguely expressed. Those who are most cultured divide the year into fourteen months, each one being of twenty days, some intercalary days being then added at the end of each month. July, which they call *Satz-tzi-mitl*, is the first month in their year; in addition to its twenty days, it has as many intercalary days as there are days on which soles, tunny-fish, cod, bream, and so forth, continue to be abundant. The month which follows and which corresponds to part of our August, is called *Tza-quetl-chigl*, and rarely has any intercalary days. *Inic-coat-tzi-mitl* is the month devoted to the felling of timber, and as for the felling of timber they partially burn the trunk of the tree at the bottom, the name of the month includes the word *inic*, which means "fire." In the months of *Estz-tzatl*, *Ma-mi-tza* and *Car-la-tic*, fish are very scarce, and these three months together cover the time of such scarcity down to the beginning of winter, the rigour of which is expressed in the names of its months, *Aju-mitls*, *Bat-tzo* and *U-yaca-milks*. These months conclude about the middle of our February, when *Aya-ca-milks* begins; this month is famed for the abundance of sardines. *Pu-cu-migl* denotes that geese and ducks are plentiful; the following month, *Ca-ya-milks*, is that in which the most important events take place; it is the season of whale fishing and is the time when whale grease for the whole year is collected. In *Ca-hutz-mitl* and *Atz-etz-milt*, fruits, roots and vegetables are in season and are gathered, and of these two months, the end of the latter almost exactly corresponds to the summer solstice.

A kind of chronology, by which the natives date their acts, is also supplied by the reigns of the taises, but since these are calculated according to their ordinary method of reckoning time, the same uncertainty prevails and there are a thousand difficulties to be met before the date of the settlement of Nootka can be discovered. The task is, indeed, impossible except for some one who should have knowledge of their language and a perfect understanding of their manners and customs.

If, after all that has been said of the natives of Nootka, an attempt were to be made to estimate their capacity and character, according to our own experience of them and according to information received from others, it must be said that among them many can be found who have good understanding and a lively imagination, and that many of them are docile, anxious to act rightly, honest and willing to oblige. The readiness with which they understand that which is explained to them, their accuracy in imitating our actions, their skill in expressing themselves by signs when Spanish words fail them, and the many objects which they make, are indications of their ability. Their pleased looks when they met our people, the cordiality with which they treated us when we went to their houses, and the prompt manner in which they fulfilled our demands or requests, show their docility. Macuina noticed that the commandant Eliza was short of supplies of food for his own table and for his men, and at once ordered his Mischimis to bring fish to him every day, accepting nothing in return, and finding that the commandant was accustomed to eat meat, of which he then had none, he sent him a carcase of venison almost every week. He visited this officer most frequently when he knew that he was most in want of supplies. The commandant Quadra, who was resident at Nootka for a whole summer, states in his diary that he never had cause to complain of the natives; he praises the confidence with which they slept in his house, and the way in which Macuina even slept in the same corner as he did, without showing the least concern. When night overtook them at the station, and it was necessary for them to go back to their own village to sleep, they asked frankly for torches to light them on their way, and returned them on the following morning. The strongest proof of their sense of justice and of the fact that they regulate their conduct by its precepts is, however, to be found in the punctuality with which they discharged all their undertakings. The chief Natzapé on one occasion asked various men belonging to the packet-boat *San Carlos* for some sheets of copper and other articles as a loan, that he might take them to the Nuchimases and barter them for skins; his canoe unfortunately capsized and he had the sorrow to lose his wife, to whom he was tenderly attached, his own goods and those which he had with him belonging to other persons. It may seem that in such sad circumstances he could have been excused from paying his creditors, but in conformity with his ideas of right dealing, this chief took upon himself the whole burden of his adverse fortune and worked incessantly in order to pay in full that which he owed.

The delight with which the natives received Valdés, Salamanca and Vernaci when they arrived in the schooners at Nootka, remembering the intercourse which they had had with them during the previous year when they were on board the corvettes *Descubierta* and *Atrevida*, and the eagerness with which they asked for news of the commanders of those vessels, shows that they are capable of feeling friendship and gratitude, unless it is to be supposed that self-interest was the sole motive for those signs of both feelings which they exhibited. They displayed remarkable affection for Don Pedro Alberni, captain of volunteers, although he had left the station and was not to return to it. Mosiño says that when he said good-bye to them on his return to San Blas, the chief Nanaquius begged him to embrace Alberni many times on his behalf and to assure him of his tender affection.

CHAPTER XX

The schooners leave Nootka; the wind drives them out to sea and they are unable to approach the land until they reach 47° north.—They survey Eceta Entry and follow the line of the coast until they reach the points already surveyed by the corvettes *Descubierta* and *Atrevida*.—They sight Cape Mendocino and anchor at Monterey.—Directions for making this harbour, and description of the character of fertility of the immediately surrounding country.—Brief account of the condition of this colony in 1792.

As the season of favourable weather was now drawing to a close, our wish to explore the coast from Fuca Strait to Monterey and San Blas led us to hasten the refitting of our ships and the performance of such other tasks as had to be completed before we could continue our voyage. On the thirty-first the bottoms of both vessels were examined and were found to be in no need of repair, and we made ready to set sail on the following night, availing ourselves of the land breeze. We hoisted sail at two o'clock, the wind blowing freshly from the north and the sky being clear, but the wind gradually fell and when day broke we had not even reached Rocky Point.

In the course of the day the weather began to change for the worse, and at sunset we were still within sight of the coast of Nootka, at 49° 13′ north. In the night a strong east wind sprang up, obliging us to tack on a southerly course in order that we might not be driven away from the coast which we wished to follow and to map as far as Monterey. The sea and the wind, however, were against us and carried us so far out that on the fourth, at midday, we were at 48° 20′ north and forty leagues from the shore. We steered towards it and approached it at 47° north, standing in to the mouth of a harbour discovered by the American, Captain Gray, and having little depth at its entrance; as night came on, we did not examine it and tacked past it in order that we might not miss Eceta Entry.

Morning found us off a low-lying shore, from which a cape ran out to the south-west; we supposed this to be San Roque, the northern point of the entry which had been visited by Don Bruno Eceta, lieutenant of the navy, in command of the frigate *Santiago*, on 17 August 1775, and named by him Asuncion Entry. It was advisable to explore this place, as many navigators had questioned its existence and Captain Vancouver, who had visited the coast very near this point, had said that there could be no considerable entry on the whole coast from 45° north to Fuca Strait. We steered for Cape San Roque, having thirteen fathoms under us, and found that the water became much shallower as we approached land, so that when we came close to the cape we found bottom at three fathoms. When we had doubled the cape, we saw a creek and an entry, three miles wide at its end; the roughness of the water, the appearance of currents and the fact that the entry was shallow led us to feel sure that it was a bar at the mouth of a river. As we approached it, however, we found that the lay of the land agreed with that given in a map drawn by that energetic navigator, the American, Mr. Gray, of a river which he called Columbia, after the frigate which he commanded. We found a depth of from three to five fathoms in the entry, and as soon as we were a little distance from Cape San Roque, towards the south, we made certain that the place which we had in sight was identical with Eceta Entry, since the cape appeared to be an island and this was one of the characteristics noted by Don Bruno Eceta as marking the entry which he had discovered. As the land within the creek between Capes San Roque and Frondoso is very low, we were not surprised that the entry, seen from a distance, should have appeared to be of considerable size. Eceta calculated that it lay at 46° 9′ north; we found that Cape Frondoso was almost exactly on the same parallel as the entry, and that it was at 46° 14′ north. Our marine clock gave its longitude as 2° 30′ 30″ east of Nootka.

Having settled the doubts to which this discovery had given rise, and taking into consideration the weakness and bad sailing qualities of our ships, we would not spend more time on this coast than was necessary in order to fix the situation of its chief points. We steered very close to it, however, and succeeded in charting that part of it which lies between 46° 8′ north and 46° 35′ north. We saw Bad Weather Cape, so named by Captain Cook, and to the south of it an opening, towards which we made; on coming to within two lengths of the shore, we found that the channel was very narrow and impracticable. After this, the weather became so bad and the wind was so strong that we were carried so far out to sea that we could not sight any other point on the coast, except Cape Mendocino on the twentieth, and on the twenty-third we anchored at Monterey.

It was with great satisfaction that we landed on the fertile shore of this settlement, the chief of our settlements in California, and the delight of our crews was still greater, since they were exhausted with continuous labour, and by the cramped and uncomfortable conditions on the ships, so that, despite the fact that they were all in the best of health, they sighted this harbour of refuge with a pleasure which can be guessed. We now considered that the dangers which are encountered in high latitudes were at an end, and that the lie had been given to those sad forebodings which had been felt at San Blas and Acapulco concerning the expedition of the schooners, on the ground that they were not vessels suited for such an undertaking.

We spent the period of our stay at Monterey in drawing the map of the explorations which had been made from the time of our leaving Nootka to that of our arrival in this harbour. Lack of space on board ship had prevented us from drawing the results of each day's exploration on paper with any completeness, and we had confined ourselves to noting the essential details very clearly in order that we might be able afterwards to form a single chart and to fill in details when we had opportunity and conditions enabling us to do so. No more suitable time could have been found than that of our stay at Monterey, and so we made such use of it that by the twentieth of October we had completed and expanded in detail the most important part of our observations.

Monterey harbour is situated at 36° 35′ 45″ north and 111° 47′ 30″ east of Cadiz, according to the careful calculations which we made in conjunction with other naval officers on board the corvettes *Descubierta* and *Atrevida* in 1791. It affords a pleasant port of call both for ships sailing from the Philippines to San Blas and Acapulco and for those which are returning to those harbours after having visited the north-west coast of America. Owing, however, to the thick mist which almost always covers the coast, the navigator who wishes to make this port is obliged to exercise care. The best way of making it is to pick up a point a mile from Cape New Year and then to navigate in the direction of Pine Cape, passing it at a league's distance and steering towards the end of the creek, where it is possible to anchor in fourteen fathoms. If when Cape New Year has been sighted the coast is covered with mist, it is well to proceed under little sail towards the harbour, taking soundings from time to time in order to make sure that the right course is being followed, and when near enough to hear the guns of the fort, lights should be shown over the side which will be answered from the fort, thus supplying sufficient indication of the direction and distance. It is also important to remember that at full and new moon high tide is at half-past one and the rise eight feet.

The land round the harbour is undulating and consists of rich and fertile ground. The earth is black, and at a depth of one or two feet there is a sandy and gravelly subsoil, except close to the sea, the shores of which are in general composed of banks of shifting sand. There is at Monterey no lack of water, as is the case elsewhere in California; it has woods, groves, abundant pasture and a number of medicinal herbs. The land is very suitable for the growing of wheat, maize, roots and vegetables. In the mission of San Carlos, fruit is not abundant all the year round, but in that of Santa Clara, twenty leagues distant, it is as abundant as it is sweet at all seasons. The constant mists, which are a source of difficulty to those who approach the harbour from the sea, are beneficial for the inhabitants, since, while they are not prejudicial to health, they temper the heat of the sun in summer, irrigate the soil, and make it fertile, in such a manner as to produce a pleasing illusion, the land in the month of August being not arid but covered with the verdure of spring.

Many bears are found in the vicinity; they are like those of Europe. There are deer, hares, squirrels and, above all, rabbits; the last multiply in such numbers that they can be sometimes caught with the hand. Among birds, the commonest are ducks, pigeons, geese, partridges, sparrows and quails, the last being very lovely and of the kind called by naturalists *Tetrao de Californias*.

The beaches, although they are not the richest so far as the variety of the shells and snails found is concerned, are so in respect of the beauty and value of those shells which are found in the greatest abundance and which naturalists call *Aliatis Myde*. The largest are sometimes as great as a bow formed by joining the thumbs and first fingers, and are covered within by a thick coating of mother-of-pearl, which is sometimes of a most vivid blue, this being the most valuable variety. We do not know of any coast so rich in this form of wealth, except that of New Zealand.

A large number of whales frequent the coast and even come into the anchorage, but the naturalist Don Francisco Mosiño and the English captain Matthew Weathered, a very experienced whaler, declare that they are not the species from which most whale grease is procurable, and that from the head of one of them two ounces of sperm oil can sometimes be obtained. Various kinds of fish are also caught here, and at certain seasons large shoals of sardines visit these shores.

Stock, both large and small, brought here from New Spain, has done well and increased considerably, becoming in several cases half as numerous again in the course of a year.

The residence of the governor, which is near the sea to the south-east of the harbour, consists of a square space enclosed by a low wall, within which are the houses of the employees. Monterey is the principal presidency of New California, and is the residence of the military commander of all the settlements in that region; the commander is generally a lieutenant-colonel. He has under his command a lieutenant and an ensign, and seventy-three mounted men, who constitute the garrison of this harbour. The majority of them are married men and occupy separate houses, which are small as are their families. The absence of other colonists has compelled these men to engage in all the arts and occupations which are necessary for the life of a civilised people. A small number of these soldiers suffices to put to flight whole troops of Indians if they attack the missions or if it be resolved to punish them for having committed some act of treachery or other grave offence, and there is no soldier who has any objection to taking messages to other presidencies when occasion demands, although he has to cross mountains and valleys occupied by a hostile people.

These excellent soldiers, who are also valuable colonists, live, however, always with the unhappy thought that when their strength is no longer equal to the performance of their military duties they are not permitted to settle in the place and to devote their attention to the cultivation of the soil. The prohibition laid upon the building of houses and the cultivation of lands in the immediate neighbourhood of the presidency appears to be directly opposed to all considerations of the utility, security and prosperity of the settlement, and contrary to the system which would be dictated by an enlightened policy.

Were the soldiers of the presidency, during their time of service, permitted to employ their savings and their spare time in creating a farm and raising stock, for the convenience and advantage of their families, and in order to have some provision against want when, owing to some misfortune or to old age, they can no longer serve, it is very probable that within a few years there would be a flourishing colony here, which would be a source of great profit to the residents and a great advantage for Spanish navigators. With what zeal and energy these good soldiers would devote themselves to the development of their little holdings, the product of their sweat and the only hope of their families!

Near the seashore and some two leagues from the presidency lies the mission of San Carlos, which was founded in 1770 and which is administered by three missioners from the college of San Fernando at Mexico; one of the fathers is the president of all the missions of New California. These religious have won the esteem and appreciation of all who have had occasion to come into contact with them, and to know the austerity of their life and the diligence and loving zeal with which they devote themselves to doing everything to improve the lot of the natives in every way. By their gentle behaviour, by flattery and by gifts, they succeed in attracting the natives to them and in persuading them to live near them; they are then instructed in the pursuit of agriculture and in knowledge of those mechanical arts which are most necessary for human life. It was with great satisfaction that we saw these children of nature being brought to feel a remarkable enthusiasm and love towards our religious, to whom they owe so happy a lot, if that which they enjoy be compared with that of their compatriots who live a nomad life, who are without the illumination of religion and who lack all the knowledge and all the advantages which a social life gives to mankind.

The Indians attached to this mission come either from the tribes of the Runsienes or Eslenes, which are the principal tribes in this district, or from those of the Ismuracanes or Aspaniaques. They are of medium height, dark in colour, and seem to be the slowest witted, as they are the ugliest and dirtiest, of all the natives of America. But while we must confess that stupidity is very common among them, we do not wish to suggest that they are incapable of work demanding reflection and judgment. Their stupidity seems to be rather the result of torpor due to the fact that they have not used the faculties which they possess, than of any actual limitation of these faculties, and so when they are called upon to use their intelligence and when ideas are implanted in them, they are not unable to learn and understand that which they are taught. They till the soil, look after stock, build houses and make tools, performing all the ordinary tasks of a carpenter.

Their method of hunting is extremely ingenious. They keep with great care the horns and some part of the head of a deer and fill it with dried grass, thus giving it the shape of the living animal. When they go hunting they carry these images on their heads, and having reached some suitable spot, go along on three feet, using their left hands to support them, while in their right hand they have a bow and arrow ready. As soon as they see one of these animals and know of which sex it is, they imitate the motions of the animal of the opposite sex with such perfection that the thoughtless beast is attracted within range; they then discharge their arrows with great accuracy.

Their laziness is sometimes so great that they cannot be moved to go on with work committed to them either by the hope of receiving presents or by the expectation that they may be able to live well for some days and obtain clothes with which to cover themselves. When there is great need in the presidency for material for building purposes, information is conveyed to the savage tribes in the neighbourhood, and they are told that if any Indian is prepared to engage in this labour, he will be given a cloak and a daily supply of cooked flesh and maize for his support. Many accept the offer and are ready to engage in the work; the most suitable are chosen, and on the appointed day these are brought before the governor; they hand over to him their bows and arrows, are given their cloaks and set to work.

The huts of the Indians are situated to the north-east of the hospital or mission-house, on a pleasant slope; they consist of a small circular stone or mud building covered with branches or straw. When we wished to know why it was that the Indians did not give more attention to their huts and provide themselves with houses which would be a real protection against the inclemency of the weather, the president of the mission told us that so far were the natives from wishing to have anything of the kind, that they preferred to live in the open country.

Up to the present it has been the custom in the mission to oblige the Indians to work for the common good without any division of property. This system seemed to be more in accordance with the idea of brotherhood and unity which should prevail in so limited a society, while it had also been found that those to whom some piece of land had been assigned cared very little for its cultivation and soon abandoned it entirely. The prevalent system demands some consideration, and it may at some future date be very helpful for the progress of the settlement to create among the Indians the sense of land ownership and to instil into them the idea of succession to property, in order that they may be the more stimulated to labour and industry.

The natives who are attached to the mission of San Carlos have an unusual custom. They dig a circular ditch in the earth and then cover it with a kind of bell-shaped erection, leaving a very narrow entrance rather like an oven door. On one side of this ditch they pile up wood which they eventually light. When the men come back from work, they go to this oven, where the fire has already burnt up sufficiently, and as many as can enter it, those who have to wait meanwhile amusing themselves with various games. Those who are within suffer as extreme heat as if they had been in a stove, and come out sweating copiously; they then proceed to bathe in the river, afterwards stretching themselves out on the sand and turning over and over many times. We have not been able to discover whether they do this in order to preserve their health or as a means by which to regain the strength which they have lost through excessive labour.

The value of these missions will be readily appreciated from any account of them, and they alone constitute a most convincing and weighty argument in favour of the conduct of the Spaniards and in contradiction of those charges which have been brought against them by foreigners, sometimes from jealousy, sometimes because it is the custom to do so, and generally from sheer ignorance.

CHAPTER XXI

Further information acquired at Monterey.—Mode of life, manners and customs of the tribes, the Eslenes and the Runsienes, who inhabit New California.

FROM the information which our missionaries have been able to collect concerning the two tribes, the Eslenes and the Runsienes, who occupy the whole of northern California, it appears that the former are the more numerous and that both tribes are nomadic and live in scattered groups. They owe some shadowy allegiance to certain principal chiefs, who, by reason of their greater valour and skill in war, have reduced the others to a position of subordination and obedience.

Men and women go naked, feeding in the fields like brute beasts or gathering seeds for the winter, and engaging also in hunting and fishing. Although some of these natives have now been reduced to obedience and form part of the mission of San Carlos, they still preserve their former disposition and customs, and among other habits which they retain it has been noticed that in their leisure moments they will lie on the ground face downwards for whole hours with the greatest content.

Their wars are waged with little energy and do not last long; the truces which they conclude are equally little, sure and stable. Memory of some old antipathy or perhaps some new caprice suffices to produce hostilities. We here transcribe that which the editor of the *Noticia de California*, of Father Venegas, says concerning the natives of the more southerly parts of California, since their character seems to be similar to that of these tribes:

"Their self-control is in exact proportion to their slight understanding, and none of their passions have great strength. They have no ambition, and their greatest desire is to be regarded rather as fierce than as brave. They have little or no idea of the object of ambition, which is honour, or perhaps esteem, credit, fame or a good name, or proof of superiority, as given by dignity acquired or by some form of employment. They know none of these things, and so this powerful incentive has with them no value or use, although in this life it is the motive of so many good and of so many evil deeds. The most that is detected among them is some sense of jealousy and rivalry; they like to find themselves praised or rewarded above their fellows, and by this alone are they roused to display some energy and to lay aside that sloth which is habitual with them. In their

Carved board found at Canal de la Tabla

hearts there is little trace of that canker of avarice by which so many have been corrupted and destroyed. Their wishes extend only to a desire to have food for the day without exerting themselves too much, and they take no thought for the morrow; they aspire only to possess those few miserable baubles which they use as ornaments, to fish, to hunt and to fight. Finally, their greed for landed property and for other belongings is that of men who have neither house nor hearth, who have no cultivated fields, who know nothing of the division or partition of property, and who recognise no title to possession other than that held by whoever may be the first to gather those fruits which the earth produces of herself.

"This mental attitude produces in them an extraordinary slackness and languor, so that they pass their lives in perpetual inaction and idleness, and regard any work and exertion with horror. It equally inclines them to turn to the first thing which they see or which is pointed out to them, and to change their resolution with the same readiness. They receive with indifference any good which is done to them, and it is useless to expect that they will retain any sense of gratitude. They feel hatred and enmity, and they proceed to wreak vengeance for the slightest causes, but with the same reason or for no reason they become quiet again when their vengeance has been satisfied or even when it has not been. It is enough for those whom they attack to resist them for them to abandon their revenge, since, while they pride themselves upon bravery, it may be said that there is among them no trace of real courage. Their enmity only lasts until they meet some one stronger than themselves. Anything is enough to fill them with fright, and they have no shame in abandoning that which they have undertaken and in allowing fear to have the mastery over them; on the other hand, there is no limit to their pride if they win some advantage or if their enemy is intimidated and shows weakness. . . ."

They always attack suddenly or treacherously, but few are killed in any encounter, since, when two or three have fallen, the rest run away, and they return to their original false friendship, to their pow-wows, their feasts, dances and games. Sometimes disputes between different tribes are decided by a duel; a day and place are fixed, the chiefs send word to their subjects, and the latter assemble with bows, arrows and shields, their bodies painted red and adorned with feathers. Their wives and children generally follow them, but take the precaution of remaining at some distance from the place of battle, in order to be more easily able to take to flight or to share in the celebration of victory, according as to whether the result of the conflict be adverse or favourable. They are accustomed to enter into battle chanting martial songs mingled with strange cries, and the combatants form themselves into two lines very close together before beginning to shoot their arrows. As one of their chief resources is to intimidate the enemy, each side wishes to let the other see its preparations for battle, and for the same reason they inflict the most horrible cruelties upon the first victims.

We have been able to acquire very little information concerning the religious ideas of the Eslenes and Runsienes, whether because those ideas are rudimentary or because the missionaries have perhaps shown their disgust on hearing an account of their belief, and they have thus become frightened and silent. We only succeeded in learning that the Runsienes believe that the sun has the same nature as their own, so that it can assume human form in order to kill them, and that the Eslenes believe that after death they are all transformed into *tecolotes*, owls—birds which they hold in marked veneration.

Among the Runsienes and Eslenes, no man is allowed to have more than one wife. The Runsienes do not punish their wives for unfaithfulness, but inflict blows, wounds or cuts on the body of the adulterer, these sometimes costing him his life. Among the Eslenes divorce was common, but it was their custom to make them go, or rather to hand them over, to their new lovers; these were obliged to compensate the former husbands for the expense to which they would be put in securing a new wife.

The custom of purchasing wives was common to both tribes, although among the Runsienes the contract was rendered far more solemn by the fact that the relatives of the parties took part in it, those of the husband contributing a share of the cost, which was divided among the relatives of the bride at the time when she was handed over.

The women of both tribes show praiseworthy tenderness in their care for their children, for whose sake they undergo the greatest dangers and labours. The women of California are in general fertile and robust, and it is not uncommon to see them give birth to a child in a field and to return to work as soon as the newly born baby is out of their care.

Theft is a crime almost unknown among these two tribes. Among the Runsienes homicide is regarded with indifference, but this is not so among the Eslenes, who punish murder with death. The funeral ceremonies of these two nations, on the death of a chief, were not the same but appeared to be so. The whole tribe gathered to make lamentations round the corpse; they tore their hair and cast ashes on their heads. This ceremony, which lasted sometimes for four days, was followed by the burial, the dead man being interred with some clothes and ornaments.

The Runsienes ultimately divided among the relatives of the deceased the few possessions which he may have left; the Eslenes, on the contrary, did not distribute anything, but all the friends and subjects of the dead chief were compelled to contribute some ornaments, which were buried with the corpse.

The same degree of difference which has been described as being found in the manners and customs of these two tribes appears also in their language, as will be seen from a comparison of the words given below:

	Eslen.	Runsien.
One	Pek	Enjalá.
Two	U-lhaj	Ultis.
Three	Julep	Kappes
Four	Jamajus	Ultizim
Five	Pe-majalá	Hali-izú
Six	Pegualanai	Hali-shakem
Seven	Jula-jualanní	Kapkamai-shakem
Eight	Julep-jualanai	Ultuamai-Shakem
Nine	Jamajus-jaulamai	Pakke.
Ten	Tomoila	Tam-chajt
Water	Azanax	Ziy
Friend	Mish-fe	Kauk
Bow	Payunaj	Laguan
Sky	Imita	Terraj
Little	Ojusk	Pishit
Day	Asatzá	Ishmen
Arrow	Lottos	Teps
Fire	Ma-mamanes	Hello
Large	Putuki	Ishac
Son	Panna	Enshinsh
Daughter	Tapanna	Kaana
Man	Ejennutek	Muguyamk
Brother	Mi-itz	Taan
Moon	Yomanis-ashi	Orpetuei-ishmen
Light	Jetza	Shorto
Woman	Tanutek	Latriyamank
Mine	Nistchá	Ka
Mother	Azia	Aán
Night	Tomanis	Orpetuei
Father	A-hay	Appan
Yours	Nimetahá	Me

CHAPTER XXII

The schooners leave Monterey, and owing to bad weather are unable to survey the coast until they arrive at the channel of Santa Barbara, the islands in which they examine.—They enter the harbour of San Diego and continue along the coast to 27° 30′ north, when they leave it in order to examine the Alixos reefs.—They stand in to shore at Cape San Lucas and finally anchor in the harbour of San Blas, where, the expedition being ended, these vessels are handed over.

ON the twenty-second of October we were ready to set sail, but the wind was steady in the north and we could not do so. On the twenty-fifth it became favourable, and at two on the morning of the twenty-sixth we set out, with the wind in the second quarter. Its force carried us out to sea and we shaped our course southwards. On the twenty-seventh, with a light north-westerly wind, we steered towards the channel of Santa Barbara, and when we were near it, it was decided that the schooner *Mexicana* should proceed to the north and the *Sutil* to the south of the islands formed by it.

On the twenty-ninth, in the morning, we sighted the Lobos reef; we coasted along the islands of San Anaclero and San Miguel and examined that of Santa Barbara, keeping close to its shore and making a definite observation of its latitude. On the thirty-first we were in a line with the north-west point of the island of Santa Catalina, and proceeding alongside it out to sea, we reached the extreme southerly point of the island at the end of the harbour. The length of the island of San Andres was geometrically determined.

The night was calm, and day broke with insufficient wind for us to continue along the shore, on which account we proceeded towards the harbour of San Diego, having already determined the position of all these islands which are of regular altitude; by the island of Santa Catalina there are two anchorages of fair safety. We did not make any direct observations in order to determine the latitude and longitude of the island of San Nicolas, since they had been determined in the previous year by the corvettes *Descubierta* and *Atrevida*.

A threatening sky led us to fear that there would be a change in the weather, which up to this time had been very favourable. We were in the evening in sight of the coast, and when night, which was stormy, had passed, we proceeded at dawn towards Point San Diego, the latitude and longitude of which we were anxious to determine. We passed near it through the weed which lies all round it, and keeping a look out for the reef which runs out to the south; as soon as we had doubled it, we sighted the corvette *Concepcion*, which we had left at Nootka; a canoe came over from her, with the naval ensign Don Juan Matute, in order to supply us with various pieces of information which might be useful to us.

On entering the bay, we kept close to the west coast, in view of the fact that the reefs on the east coast make the entrance of the harbour difficult to negotiate. As it was our intention by midday to be off Point San Diego, in order to observe its latitude, we tacked there from the anchorage and made the desired observation with complete success, the sun being at its highest. The weather becoming more favourable, we pursued our voyage so as to pass between the Coronados and the shore, and to prepare a chart of as much of the coast as lies between Point San Diego and 32° 10′ north. We did not undertake to do more than to fix the principal points on the coast; in order to do this without changing our direct course, we ran on the fourth from 31° 35′ north to 31° 20′ north; on the fifth from 30° 30′ north to 29° 45′ north; on the sixth we passed along as much of the gulf or indentation of the coast as lies between Point Canoe and Cape Santa Maria, and on the seventh we traversed the strait formed by the island of La Navidad and the shore. Our labours ended at 27° 40′ north in a creek where there is a good anchorage with a sandy bottom, and which is possibly the harbour which was called San Bartolome by Sebastian Vizcaino.

We should have continued along the coast to Cape San Lorenzo had it not been that our attention was drawn to a more interesting matter. The maps corrected by the officers and pilots belonging to the department of San Blas, place at 25° north the reefs called Alixos, and according to other information supplied by the commander of the frigate *San Andrés*, who sighted them on arriving off this coast on a voyage from the Philippines, these islets lie at 24° 34′ north. Having decided to examine into this point, we shaped our course so as to be at the supposed latitude of the reefs, and were twenty leagues west of them in the evening. From here the *Mexicana* proceeded on 24° 56′ north, and the *Sutil* on 24° 30′ north, a rendezvous being fixed at 24° 30′ north, and 208° 30′ west of Cadiz. During the night we were able only to make the twelve miles for which we could see at nightfall; having completed this distance, we hove to for the rest of the night. But what was our surprise when, on taking our observations at midday on the following day, we found ourselves a considerable distance farther south, as a result of which fact we failed to make the position on which we had determined, and had no course open to us but to proceed westward and explore along 24° 30′ north. At two on the morning of the thirteenth, the schooners rejoined one another at the appointed place, and we were able only to certify that the Alixos were not situated where they had been placed by the frigate *San Clemente*, and that consequently the position given to them by the observers from San Blas was to be rather accepted. The corvette *Concepcion*, which we left in the harbour of San Diego, was more fortunate, and the observations of her commander established that the said islets were in that position which had been originally assigned to them.

The schooners, having rejoined one another, steered towards Cape San Lucas; the wind was strong from the west-north-west and the weather fine, so that on the morning of the fifteenth the shore of the extreme south of the peninsula of California was sighted. At midday we were parallel with the Cape, and on comparing its real longitude with that indicated by our Arnold clock, number 344, we found that there were thirteen minutes' difference, this error having occurred since the clock had been last regulated in the harbour of Monterey. It was accordingly necessary to correct the longitudes which we had determined to this extent.

We steered for the Maria Islands, of which we wished to fix the latitude and longitude, although astronomical observations had been made in sight of them during the previous year by our friends of the corvettes *Descubierta* and *Atrevida*. On the eighteenth a sail was sighted to the west, and at midday she came up with us; she was the corvette *Concepcion*, commanded by the naval lieutenant, Don Francisco de Eliza, who did us the honour of keeping with us, shortening sail considerably in view of the superior speed of his vessel. Availing ourselves of steady winds, we stood on our course; in the evening of the twentieth, the wind became stronger, and enabled us to sight at nightfall the peaks of the island of Concepcion, the most north-easterly of these islands of Maria.

On the twenty-first we observed the latitude of the most northerly part of this island, but the calms and currents did not permit us to continue the work which would have been necessary in order to draw an exact map of the island. At one o'clock at night we experienced a squall which placed us in a position of some danger; it began from the north and turned to the west, the force of the wind being so great that although the *Mexicana* had only her small sails set, she nearly capsized. The *Sutil* ran before the wind with bare poles. The wind and heavy rain extinguished all the lights, and in these circumstances we welcomed the flashes of lightning as the only means by which we could observe the compass and so manœuvre as not to run on to the islands and not to allow the three vessels to collide with one another. When the wind fell we were at a considerable distance from the land, but the schooners did not sight each other all night, this being the only occasion during the whole voyage on which they parted involuntarily. They were reunited on the morning of the twenty-second, and proceeded directly for the anchorage of San Blas, where we dropped anchor on the twenty-third. Our crews arrived in perfect health and full of delight at the happy ending of an expedition which was very laborious and full of risk, taking into consideration the kind of vessel employed upon it. The purpose for which these ships had been fitted out having been accomplished, we handed them over to the officer commanding the department, and ourselves prepared to return to Spain by way of Mexico and Vera Cruz.

INDEX

Acapulco, 4, 5, 6, 7, 8, 44, 124
Activo, brigantine, 90, 116
Aguilar, Martin del, 5
Alberni, Don Pedro, captain of infantry, 96, 121
Alder, Lieutenant William, R.N., commander of English brigantine *Tresbes*, 93
Aliponzoni Creek, 70, 71
Alixos, reefs, 136, 137
Amapala, gulf of, 5
Anchorage, The, 45
Angostura de los Comandantes, channel, 62, 63, 66, 67, 68, 70
Aransazu, frigate, 16, 24, 91
Arrecifes Point, 18, 21, 24
Astronomical and mathematical instruments carried on voyage, 10
Asuncion Entry, 122
Atrevida, corvette, 4, 81, 88, 94, 121, 124, 135, 137

Bad Weather Cape, 123
Balda Channel, 78
Baldinar Channel, 78
Banza, anchorage, 74
Berengeur de Marquina, Don Joaquin, 7
Bodega y Quadra, Don Juan de la, commandant of the department of San Blas, 6, 16, 18, 22, 23, 26, 44, 90, 91, 92, 93, 94, 98, 116, 118, 120
Boise, Cape, 87
Bonilla, island of, 38
Broughton, Lieutenant William Robert, R.N., commanding the brigantine *Chatham*, 44, 60
Brown, William, captain of English frigate *Butterworth*, 93
Bucareli Entry, 91
Buena Esperanza Inlet, 18, 22, 23
Bustamente Bay, 62
Butterworth, English frigate, 93

Caamaño, Don Jacinto, commander of frigate *Aransazu*, 91
Caamaño, entry of, 32, 33, 56
California, peninsula of, 137
Canoe Point, 136
Canonigo Bay, 74
Cardenas, anchorage, 75
Caremlo, mountain, 41
Carmelo, entry of, 32, 55, 56
Carvajal, channel of, 68, 70
Carvajal, Don Ciriaco Gonzalez, oidor of the audiencia of Mexico, 68
Cauti, chief, 77
Ceballos, island, 65
Cepeda Point, 33, 42, 43, 44, 53, 54
Cerantes, Don Antonio, pilot of the *Princesa*, 83
Cevallos, Don Ciriaco, 94
Chatham, brigantine, 44, 58, 60
Claucuad Sound, 3, 18, 34
Columbia, American frigate, 22, 90
Concepcion, corvette, 16, 91, 136, 137
Concepcion, island, 137
Concha, anchorage, 66
Consolation Creek, 87
Conuma, mountain, 109
Cook, Captain, 94, 95, 99, 101, 102, 123
Cook River, 61
Cordero, Don Joseph, cartographer to expedition to explore Juan de Fuca Strait, 9
Cordero Channel, 73
Cordoba, harbour of, 34, 35, 38
Coronados, 136
Cox, Port, 92

Daedalus, English frigate, 91, 93
Descanso Creek, 47, 51, 55
Descubierta, corvette, 4, 81, 88, 94, 121, 124, 135, 137
Discovery, corvette, 44, 58, 61

INDEX

Dixon, George, English sailor and trader, 90
Douglas, Captain, 92

Eceta, Don Bruno de, 5, 122, 123
Eceta Entry, 122
Eddy Point, 71
Eliza, Don Francisco, 3, 16, 18, 32, 120, 137
Engaño Channel, 71, 72, 73
Eslenes, tribe, 127 ; mode of life, manners and customs, 130-4 ; comparison of words used in Eslen and Runsien languages, 134
Espinosa, Don Joseph de, 94
Estero Creek, 71
Ezera Sound, 33, 56, 81

Feliz Aventurero, Portuguese packet-boat, 92, 93
Fidalgo, Don Salvador, commander of corvette *Princesa*, 25, 26, 27, 29
Flavia, French frigate, 19
Flon, entry of, 32, 33, 56
Flores Bay, 74
Floridablanca Sound, 32, 33, 42, 43, 45, 52, 54, 55, 56, 57, 61
Friendly Cove, 95
Frondoso, Cape, 15, 85, 87, 105, 123

Galiano, Don Dionisio Alcalá, commander of expedition to explore Juan de Fuca Strait, 5, 9, 58, 60, 62, 66, 86
Galvez, Luis, leach in the *Aransazu*, 24
Garton Bay, 32, 33, 40, 41
Garzon, creek of, 42
Gaviola, Point, 47
Gertrudis, frigate, 16, 19
Good Hope Bay, 94
Gorostiza Harbour, 86
Gray, Captain, commanding American frigate *Columbia*, 22, 90, 122, 123
Guemes, channel of, 39, 54, 84, 85 ; island of, 39, 40

Hope, American brigantine, 93
Horcasitas, schooner, 3

Insult, anchorage, 75
Istocoti-Clemoc, daughter of Macuina, 112, 113
Izmitz, 109, 110

Juan de Fuca Strait, 3, 4, 5, 24, 28, 44, 56, 81, 83, 90, 92, 122, 123 ; words spoken on the southern branch of, 36-7 ; native names of various points on, 37

King George's Harbour, 94

La Navidad, island, 136
La Separación, anchorage, 61
Langara, Point, 43, 44, 52, 53, 54, 55
Lanz, Cape, 87
Lara, creek of, 41
Lobos Reef, 135

Macuina, chief, 15, 16, 16, 18, 22, 23, 74, 77, 90, 92, 100, 102, 104, 105, 110, 112, 113, 116, 117, 118, 120
Macuina, Point, 15, 105
Mage, James, captain of American frigate *Margaret*, 93
Majoa, settlement of, 83, 85
Malaspina Bay, 62
Maldonado, Captain Lorenzo Ferrer, 4
Malvinas, 17
Manila, 7, 9
Manuel de Alvala, Don Joseph, 8
Margaret, American frigate, 93
Maria, wife of chief Tetacus, 28, 29
Maria Islands, 65, 137
Marlox, 109
Martinez, Don Estéban, 3, 92, 95
Mathematical and astronomical instruments carried on voyage, 10
Matute, Don Juan, naval ensign, 136
Maurell, Don Francisco, 4
Mazaredo, entry of, 32, 54, 55, 58
Meares, Captain, 80, 104

INDEX

Mendocino, Cape, 123
Mexicana, schooner, 5, 8, 12, 13, 16, 24, 29, 34, 41, 46, 59, 60, 62, 65, 68, 71, 78, 82, 86, 135, 136, 137; dimensions of, 9; armament of, 9; astronomical and mathematical instruments carried, 10
Mier, anchorage, 86
Mischimis, 18, 22, 23, 108, 109, 110, 111, 113, 114, 116, 117, 120
Monterey, 122, 123, 124, 125, 126, 137
Monterey shells, 27, 49, 102
Moreno de la Vega, Point, 34
Mosiño, Don Francisco, naturalist, 95, 98, 121, 125
Mulgrave Harbour, 75
Murphy, anchorage, 66

Nanaquius, chief, 117, 118, 121
Narvaez, Don Joseph, pilot, 4
Natzapé, chief, 117, 120
New Whirlpools Channel, 74
News, Thomas, commander of frigate *Daedalus*, 91
Nitimar, Point of, 24, 25
Nootka (Nuqueño), language of, 26, 34, 74, 75, 77, 78, 89, 115
Nootka, natives of, 98–121; general appearance, ornaments and dress, 98–101; weapons, 101; houses, 101–2; food, 102; question of cannibalism, 102–4; arts and occupations, 105–7; government, 107–8; religion and beliefs, 108–9; funeral rites, 109–10; hereditary dignity of tais, 110–11; polygamy, marriage, etc., 111–14; evils introduced by Europeans, 115; language and method of counting, 115–16; eloquence, 116–18; poetry, music and dancing, 118–19; chronology, 119–20; capacity and character, 120–1
Nootka (Nuqueño) Island, 26, 94, 95, 96, 110, 115, 120, 121, 122, 123

Nootka Sound, 3, 4, 15, 17, 19, 23, 24, 26, 27, 28, 29, 34, 39, 44, 82, 83, 88, 91, 92, 94
Notkeños, 18
Novales, anchorage, 74
Novales Channel, 72
Nuchimases, 76, 77, 79, 109, 117, 120
Nuñez Gaona, harbour of, 25, 92
Nuqueño (Nootka) Island, 26
Nuqueño (Nootka) language, 26, 34, 74, 75, 77, 78, 89, 115

Olavinde Channel, 73
Our Lady of Rosario, channel of, 32

Pacheco, channel of, 41
Perez, Don Juan, commanding frigate *Santiago*, 94
Perouse, Count de la, 19,
Philippine Islands, 6, 124
Pinelo Channel, 78
Pin-pula, 109
Porlier Entry, 45, 46, 49, 59
Prince Leo, English sloop, 93
Princesa Real, corvette, 3, 25, 26
Prince William Entry, 93
Pujet, Mr., second lieutenant of the corvette *Discovery*, 60, 61

Quacos, settlement of, 83
Quadra Harbour, 32
Quatlaza-pé, brother of chief Macuina, 17, 106, 112, 114, 117
Quautz, the Creator, 108, 109, 111, 118, 119
Queen Charlotte Island, 93
Quema, island, 59
Quicomasia, chief, 17, 18, 110, 112, 117
Quimper, Don Manuel, 3, 32
Quintano, channel of, 62, 66

Refuge Creek, 69, 70, 71
Retamal Channel, 78
Revillagigedo, Count of, *see* Viceroy of New Spain
Robredo Creek, 65

INDEX

Rocky Point, 94
Runsienes, tribe, 127; mode of life, manners and customs, 130–4; comparison of words used in Runsien and Eslen languages, 134

Salamanca, Don Secundino, lieutenant of schooner *Sutil*, 5, 9, 15, 50, 56, 62, 63, 68, 72, 73, 75, 121
Salida Harbour, 86
San Anaclero, island, 135
San Andrés, frigate, 7, 8, 9, 136
Sand Andres, island, 135
San Bartolome, harbour, 136
San Blas, 3, 5, 6, 7, 8, 18, 24, 25, 26, 54, 56, 94, 121, 122, 124, 136, 137, 138
San Carlos, mission, 125, 126, 128
San Carlos, packet-boat, 3, 34, 38, 80, 102, 120
San Clemente, frigate, 137
San Diego, harbour, 135, 137
San Diego, Point, 135, 136
San Esteban Point, 94
San Juan, island of, 38
San Lorenzo, Cape, 136
San Lorenzo Harbour, 94
San Lucas, Cape, 137
San Miguel, island, 15, 135
San Nicolas, island, 135
San Rafael, island, 15
San Rafael, Point, 42, 43
San Roque, Cape, 122, 123
Santa Barbara, island, 135
Santa Barbara Channel, 5, 81, 91, 135
Santa Catalina, island, 135
Santa Clara, mission, 125
Santa Cruz, harbour of, at Nootka, 39, 95
Santa Maria, Cape, 136
Santiago, frigate, 94, 122
Sarmiento, Point, 62
Saturnina, schooner, 38
Shepherd, Henry, captain of the *Venus*, 83, 93
Sisiaquis, chief, 77, 78

Solano, Punta de, 40
Sonsonate, 5
Sutil, Point, 86
Sutil, schooner, 4, 5, 8, 12, 13, 16, 24, 28, 29, 34, 40, 41, 44, 46, 49, 55, 58, 59, 60, 65, 68, 70, 71, 78, 82, 84, 86, 87, 135, 136, 137; dimensions of, 9; armament of, 9; astronomical and mathematical instruments carried, 10

Tabla, channel of, 61, 62
Taisoun, chief, 28
Tasis, 116
Tetacus, chief, 28, 29, 33, 34, 35, 36, 38, 42
Texada, island, 59
Tiupananulg, chief, 18, 110
Torres, Don Alonso de, 16
Torres Channel, 80
Tres Hermanos, 40
Tresbes, English brigantine, 93

Valdés, Don Cayetano, captain of schooner *Mexicana*, 5, 9, 12, 15, 24, 29, 35, 58, 60, 61, 62, 66, 74, 121
Valdés Harbour, 87
Vancouver, Captain George, R.N., commanding the corvette *Discovery*, 44, 55, 58, 60, 61, 64, 91, 92, 93, 94, 122
Venus, brigantine, 83, 93
Vera Cruz, 138
Vernaci, Don Juan, lieutenant of schooner *Mexicana*, 5, 9, 15, 34, 45, 56, 60, 62, 63, 68, 75, 76, 78, 79, 121
Viana, Don Francisco, 92
Viana Creek, 73
Viceroy of New Spain, 3, 4, 16
Villaviciencio Creek, 86
Vizcaino, Sebastian, 136

Wicananish, chief, 18, 117
Wintuysen Entries, 47, 49, 50

Yucuatl, 94, 105, 108